A PAILFUL OF STARS

A Pailful of Stars

*Gleams of Hope
for a Time of Despair*

by FRANKLIN M. SEGLER

Broadman Press / Nashville, Tennessee

Bible quotations used in this book are taken from the Revised Standard Version
unless otherwise indicated at the end of the quotation. Occasionally the author has
given his own translation.

Library of Congress Catalog Card Number: 75–178065
Dewey Decimal Number: 242
Printed in the United States of America

FOR FANNIE MAE
Cherished
Christian
Companion

CONTENTS

INTRODUCTION

"Didn't you ever search for another star?" A contemporary poet Alfred Starr Hamilton gave this title to an intriguing poem. Sensing the dark mood of Hungarian suffering, he also found laughter and riches and rhapsody in the hearts of the people. He offers hope in the following lines:

Why, I'll send you a silver key to the cave of despair
I'll send you a violet tonight, I'll send you a silver sword
I'll send you a silver hammer that'll hammer night and day
I'll send you a pailful of our kinds of blue revolutionary stars.[1]

Ours is a questioning age as Chad Walsh suggests in his book *God at Large.* In his imagination Walsh pictures a "graph of time" with irregular and surprising lines and curves which suggest confusion and perhaps doubts. The lines include warships, hippie communes, drug use, student demonstrations, rising pollution, computer production, and nuclear missiles. "Which lines are the future?" Walsh asks.

One evening as I sat at home looking out into space, our daughter Sylvia asked, "What are you doing, Daddy, gazing at the stars?" I replied, "No, just wrestling with a burden." About three o'clock the next morning I found myself awake, thinking about that same problem. As I stood before the window, I looked into the heavens and saw one bright star gleaming radiantly. Then I remembered what Sylvia had asked, and I thought, Yes, there's always one star in God's bright sky of hope. Then some of those promises I had learned began to gleam before my mind.

There is a future
And there are stars of hope
Which testify to that fact.
Poets and scientists and anthropologists and psychologists
Technologists and philosophers and preachers and housewives
Young people and the man on the street
Testify to an inner hope for a better day
A better world of tomorrow.

In his "Essay on Man" the seventeenth-century poet Alexander Pope wrote:

> Hope springs eternal in the human breast:
> Man never is, but always to be, blest.

There is a sounder basis for hope than man's feeling about it. In his action, God has established the sure foundation of hope. Peter wrote:

> Blessed be the God and Father
>   Of our Lord Jesus Christ!
> By His great mercy we have been born anew
> To a living hope through the resurrection
> Of Jesus Christ from the dead

—1 Peter 1:3

American people experience a great diversity in religious experiences. Our early history was characterized by a *puritanical* society; at present perhaps we could be called a *permissive* society; our great need is to become established as a *responsible* society.

What, me pious! Many people feel that to be religious is to be "pious." In his book *Requiem for a Lost Piety,* Edward Farley affirms the value of genuine Christian piety. A sound faith is based on three fundamental attitudes: (1) the fact of the gospel of grace and hope; (2) a responsible use of one's abilities and opportunities; and (3) a compassionate militance and willingness to risk fighting for the right, which is the good news of Jesus Christ.[2]

The title *A Pailful of Stars* suggests there are gleams of hope in our wandering world floating in confusion and darkness. Each of the meditations in this book begins with "a gleam of hope," then includes some reflections, selected pertinent biblical promises, and a brief prayer, which, hopefully, may offer some light to steer by.

Doubtless you have discovered many gems of hope in the Bible. It contains wisdom beyond all other literary sources. Modern man need not be ashamed to read God's Word, for it is truth and will lead him into the way of all truth.

> Thy word is like a deep, deep mind;
> And jewels rich and rare
> Are hidden in its mighty depths
> For every searcher there.

> —Edwin Hodder

Prayer for man is as needful as breathing. Man does not have to find reasons for praying, a philosophy of prayer, or a methodology of prayer. Prayer is the league of conscious fellowship with God.

Jacques Ellul says that God's commandment to pray is the "only reason for praying."[3] Ellul goes on to say that prayer belongs to the totality of life without any loophole, from the most superficial to the most profound, from my moral obligation to others to my participation in an affluent society. Thus prayer is not an affair of the moment. "There is the continuous woof on which is woven the warp of my occupations, my sentiments, my actions."[4]

In a sense the essays in this book are a testimony to the blessings of God in my own life. Life has been rich and full for me. Many of the biblical passages included here have supplied means of hope in life's dark hours. I have found the psalmist's words true:

> Thy word have I hid in my heart
> That I might not sin against thee.
> I will meditate on thy precepts,
> And fix my eyes on thy ways.
> I will delight in thy statutes;
> I will not forget thy word.
>
> Thy word is a lamp to my feet
> And a light to my path.
>
> Thy testimonies are my heritage forever;
> Yea, they are the joy of my heart.
> —Psalm 119:11,15–16,105,111

In prayer I have never been disappointed. To receive the things we ask for is important. To receive God when we pray is more important. We may not get the things we want, but we always find God in the experience of genuine prayer.

May this "pailful of stars" provide for you rays of hope and make life more meaningful and joyous is my prayer.

FRANKLIN M. SEGLER
FORT WORTH, TEXAS

NOTES

1. Jeof Hewitt, ed., *Quickly Aging Here: Some Poets of the 1970's* (Garden City, New York: Doubleday and Co., 1969), p. 4.

2. Edward Farley, *Requiem for a Lost Piety* (Philadelphia: Westminster Press, 1966), p. 124 f.

3. C. Edward Hopkin, trans., Jacques Ellul's *Prayer and Modern Man* (New York: Seabury Press, 1970), p. 104.

4. *Ibid.,* p. 107.

1.
GOD'S IN HIS HEAVEN

> God's in his heaven,
> All's right with the world.

So said a little girl who saw larks flying, and snails creeping, and dewy pearls glistening on the grassy hillside in Robert Browning's "Pippa Passes."

Is all right with the world?

That all depends—upon your definition, your perspective, and your own attitude.

Mere naiveté or blind optimism in our world cannot long survive. Obviously, all is not right with the world.

So long as there is war, I have no peace;
So long as there is crime, I cannot feel righteous;
So long as there is hatred, my love is incomplete;
So long as there is discrimination,
  I am not a whole person.

Shall I then become a pessimist? Since all is not right with the world, are we to conclude there is no hope for our world? Is the only alternative agnosticism or atheism? By no means!

In our world the fool still exclaims, "No God for me!" John Baillie of Edinburgh University once said that men may be atheists in the top of their minds, but in the bottom of their hearts they know better.

Wordsworth said that the world is too much with us. We are obsessed with getting and spending, creating and destroying, dominating and depersonalizing. We are often too much concerned with our own accomplishments and with protecting our own rights. Then we miss the overtones of God's creative purpose.

In the midst of a topsy-turvy world, in a merry-go-round of human disorder, we are not to assume that God is trapped on the merry-go-round. John Newton once said, "If you think you see the ark of the Lord falling, you may be sure it is due to a dizziness in your own head."

Chad Walsh acknowledges that God is a revolutionary, and that he is at work in the world today. However, he insists that God's created world still has mystery inbuilt in it. To lose sight of this fact is to make a panicky sellout to the spirit of the age.[1]

God only is God.

God is the God of history.

God is Lord over man.

God rules successfully in spite of man.

God sent his Son to redeem man.

God becomes known through redeemed man.

God offers life and hope to every man.

Neither shallow optimism nor morbid pessimism must reign in the life of modern man. What is needed is Christian realism. Originally God created man in his image. He provides the only concrete hope for the right kind of world.

Perhaps the little girl Pippa was right, "God's in his heaven, all's right with the world." Those who have eyes of faith can see the work of God in our contemporary world.

God's Word

I am the Lord your God. . . .

I brought you out of the land of Egypt. . . .

You shall love the Lord your God with all your heart.

—Deuteronomy 5:6; 6:4–5

God is our refuge and strength,
A very present help in trouble. . . .
Come, behold the works of the Lord,
How he has wrought desolations in the earth.
He makes wars to cease to the end of the earth;
He breaks the bow, and shatters the spear,
He burns the chariots with fire!
"Be still, and know that I am God.
I am exalted among the nations,
I am exalted into the earth!"
The God of Jacob is our refuge.

—Psalm 46:1,8–11

If God be for us,
Who can be against us?

—Romans 8:31

A Prayer

God of creation,
Lord of the universe,
Maker of man in your image,
Give us eyes of faith to see you
As sovereign Lord who reigns eternally
Thus will we have faith to believe
And courage to act
In our role of helping
To set the world right,
According to your eternal purposes
In Jesus Christ our Lord.

Amen.

NOTES

1. Chad Walsh, *God at Large* (New York: Seabury Press, 1971), p. 84.

2.
THE LORD OF LOVE MY SHEPHERD IS

The worship experience that particular Sunday morning in our church was for me an unusual blessing. Our choir sang "The Lord of Love My Shepherd Is" by Shelley. I had heard it many times before and recognized always that it had a good message. But this time the people who sang and played seemed inspired. They felt what they shared.

For example, our organist had recently lost her husband by a heart attack. A violin accompaniment was played by a mother and her teen-age son whose doctor-husband and father had died of cancer. One young couple in the choir had experienced prolonged pain. She had been injured in a collision which necessitated her wearing a cast and walking on crutches for an extended period of time. They continued to bring their children and were faithful in their worship during this season. Now they sang in the choir again.

Every person in the choral production that Sunday seemed to really feel the presence of the Good Shepherd. Through tear-dimmed eyes I worshiped and thanked God for his abiding presence and strength. I felt if there had been no other act of worship that morning, this one experience would have sufficed for the day.

The symbol of shepherd and sheep is a legacy from ancient times. My wife Fannie Mae, Sylvia, our daughter, and I spent the sabbatical year 1964–1965 in the Middle East. I taught in the Arab Baptist Seminary of Beirut, Lebanon. Nothing intrigued us more than the pastoral scenes which dotted the hills of ancient Palestine, especially in Jordan. Occasionally one would see a shepherd boy with his flute, sitting on a hillside, playing to the sheep, just as David did in ancient times.

When individual sheep strayed from the flock, a sharp call from the shepherd would turn it back. Sometimes a harsh tone was necessary.

In every instance the shepherd seemed to love the sheep. They usually were handled with gentleness and kindness. Not one time did we observe cruelty or harshness on the part of the shepherd. He always seemed to be concerned with the sheep's welfare. He sought out green pastures and fresh water for his flock.

Modern society is filled with rugged paths and painful experiences. The beleaguered and lonely heart of man reaches out for guidance and strength. Quite often the search for the right path is baffling. In fact, it is even dangerous. It calls for great risk. Sometimes one is afraid to take another step, lest he plant his foot in the wrong path or hit a stone of stumbling which may defeat him.

People often stray from the right path, even when it is pointed out to them. A nineteen-year-old youth, member of a large family, had strayed from the way which had been shown to him by the family. He once wrote to an older brother, "I guess I'm just the black sheep of the family." The older brother replied, "There are no black sheep. There may be straying sheep or lost sheep or needy sheep but no black sheep. Everyone is precious in the sight of the family and in God's sight."

When bodies are broken and health is gone, the inner pain is too much for an individual to bear alone. In such times it is good to know that others care. Parents care. Brothers and sisters and grandfathers and grandmothers and uncles and aunts and cousins and neighbors and friends all care. Have you not really felt another's pain as you stood by and saw the wrinkle in his brow? His pain became your pain.

Loneliness is one of life's most devastating experiences. Perhaps one has strayed and on the inside feels that he is separated from others. A bad conscience will create such separation. But loneliness is not always due to a bad conscience. Sometimes it is the desire for love and understanding and not knowing how to reach out for it.

Knowing how to touch another's hands seems a simple thing, but often the distance is too far to reach. At such a time the lonely individual longs for someone else to do the reaching. Actually, no one is ever alone. God is standing near. The Good Shepherd is watching over his lonely sheep.

God's Word

The Lord is my shepherd;
　I shall not want.
He maketh me to lie down in green pastures:
　He leadeth me beside the still waters.
He restoreth my soul:
　He leadeth me in the paths of righteousness for his name's sake.
Yea, though I walk through the valley
　Of the Shadow of Death, I will fear no evil;
For thou art with me;
　Thy rod and thy staff they comfort me.
Thou preparest a table before me
　In the presence of mine enemies:
Thou anointest my head with oil;
　My cup runneth over.
Surely goodness and mercy shall follow me
　All the days of my life:
And I will dwell in the house of the Lord forever.

　　　　　　　　　　　　　　　　　　—Psalm 23, KJV

Jesus said,

I am the Good Shepherd. I know my sheep, and my sheep know me; just as the Father knows me, and I know the Father, and I lay down my life for the sheep. . . . The Father loves me for this, because I am laying down my life that I may take it again. No man is taking it away from me. I am laying it down of my own accord. . . . My sheep listen to my voice, and I know them and they follow me. I am giving them eternal life, and they shall never perish, nor shall anyone snatch them out of my Father's hand. I and my Father are one. . . . I am come that they may have life, and have it in abundance.

—John 10:11,14–15,17–18,27–30,10b, Centenary

A Prayer

O Lord, our great Shepherd,
Like sheep we often stray,
   Sometimes deliberately.
Sensitize our hearing that we
   May readily answer thy call.
Attune our hearts to thy love
   That we may rejoice in thy presence.
Give us responsible wills that
   As mature members of the flock
We may lead the lambs up
   The right paths. Amen.

3.
JEREMIADS OR HALLELUJAHS?

Is your life filled with Jeremiads or Hallelujahs? That is, what kind of songs do you sing? Lamentations and mournful ballads or joyous celebrations? Or, perhaps, some of both are seen in your life-style and mine.

There is a kind of sadness in the folk ballads of the younger generation today. For example, Woody Guthrie's ballads express a loneliness, a cry for acceptance, a reaching out for a friendly touch. He had these deep feelings from his childhood, so says my wife Fannie Mae. They grew up in the same hometown, Okemah, Oklahoma.

The ballads of Jeremiah, prophet in the seventh century B.C., expressed similar feelings—rejection, self-deprecation, and worthlessness. The literary term Jeremiad was coined to describe the lamentations of Jeremiah.

Actually, the prophet produced both Jeremiads and Hallelujahs. His writings are rich and varied. His poetry possesses a lyrical quality, emotional power, a sensuousness and passionateness, and a revelation of changing moods and tempers. His self-disclosures are "confessions" of "the most intimate and unglossed, the most inward and authentic, of any that have been preserved from ancient times." [1]

These glimpes of the inner person of Jeremiah have been compared to the devotional writings of Paul, Augustine, Luther, Bunyan, and Pascal. His personal feelings break forth even in his narratives of the people in war. All his writings reveal a very sensitive nature, so often observable in the person of a genius.

Jeremiah's inner conflicts have two dimensions—the vertical, or his confrontation with God, and the horizontal, or his dialogues with his fellow-citizens. In his candor he debated with God and accused God of being unreliable. He even cursed the day he was born and his parents for bringing him into the world.

But God considered Jeremiah important. In fact, God had selected him for a significant role. He acknowledged that God had called him to be his spokesman to the nations (Jer. 1:4–5).

God knows a person's worth and has a plan for every life. God has need for each individual's gifts and influence.

When God called Jeremiah, he immediately protested, "I do not know how to speak, for I am only a youth" (1:6). He felt he was a weakling, a nobody, a worthless person. He had a low self-concept; he thought less of himself than he should have, and so he lived in constant conflict and emotional tension between God's concept and purpose for his life and his own low esteem of himself.

However, Jeremiah served God in spite of his conflicts. He knew he could rely on God, and he knew God's Word was true. He spoke for God, even though often he did not feel like it. He followed the dictation of his faith rather than his emotions.

Jeremiah was also capable of soaring to the heights of ecstasy as is seen in much of his writing. With the eyes of faith he saw visions of God and his kingdom which he shared in inspired writings.

He saw God's power in judgment:

Behold, he comes up like clouds,
  His chariots like the whirlwind;

His horses are swifter than eagles—
Woe to us, for we are ruined!

—Jeremiah 4:13–14

He saw God's wisdom:

How can you say, "We are wise,
And the law of the Lord is with us"?
But, behold, the false pens of the scribes
Has made it into a lie. . . .
They have rejected the word of the Lord. . . .
They have healed the wound of
My people lightly, saying,
"Peace, peace, when there is no peace."

—Jeremiah 8:8,9b,11

He shared God's compassion:

Is there no balm in Gilead?
Is there no physician there?
Why then has the health of the daughter
Of my people not been restored?
O that my head were waters,
And my eyes a fountain of tears,
That I might weep day and night
For the slain of the daughters of my people!

—Jeremiah 8:22 to 9:1

He believed in God's sovereign purpose:

If you return, I will restore you
And you shall stand before me.
Blessed is the man who trusts in the Lord, . . .
He is like a tree planted by the water. . . .
for it does not cease to bear fruit.

—Jeremiah 15:19;17:7–8

He affirmed the faithfulness of God:

Remember my affliction and my bitterness,
The wormwood and the gall!

My soul continually thinks of it
And is bowed down within me.
But this I call to mind,
And therefore have I hope:
The steadfast love of the Lord never ceases
His mercies never come to an end
They are new every morning;
Great is thy faithfulness.

—Lamentations 3:19–22

Do you identify with Jeremiah? I certainly do. Perhaps the average person feels a kinship with the ancient man of God, whose life was a sort of emotional battlefield.

Can we also identify with him in his faith? The answer for his feelings of inferiority and worthlessness was found in his trust in God. He couldn't get away from God's constant care and call in his life. He discovered his identity when he found his destiny in the God of purpose.

In a sermon, "Remembering Who We Are," John Claypool used the following pungent illustration. In his autobiographical novel, *Report to Creco,* Nikos Kazantakis tells of an earnest young man who asked a saintly old monk, "Do you still wrestle with the devil, Father?" The old man answered, "Not any longer, my son. I have grown old, and he has grown old with me. He no longer has the strength. . . . now I wrestle with God." "Do you hope to win?" the youth asked. "Oh, no, my son, I hope to lose," replied the old man.

A Prayer

Lord of ancient peoples,
You are Lord also of modern man.
Because you do not change or falter
Your purposes are stamped in our heart.
In our emotional conflicts and turmoil
Help us to be sensitive to your voice.

In our wrestling with you
May you always win.
Because you love us steadfastly,
May we learn to love ourselves.
Then we shall have the courage
   to be ourselves,
   to do your work,
   in a day when your redemption
   is the only hope for a weary world.
God of compassion, give us a few Hallelujahs
To drown out the Jeremiads in our lives. Amen.

NOTES

1. George A. Buttrick, ed., *The Interpreter's Dictionary of the Bible* (Nashville: Abingdon Press, 1962), Vol. 3, p. 824.

4.
IN SEARCH OF MIND EXPANSION

In his poem "The Everlasting Mercy" Masefield describes the feelings of a converted poacher:

Oh glory of the light and mind,
How dead I'd been, how dumb, how blind!
The station broke to my new eyes,
Was bubbling out of paradise;
The waters rushing from the rain
Were singing "Christ has risen again."
I thought all earthly creatures knelt
From rapture of the joy I felt.
The narrow station wall's brick ledge,
The wild hop withering in the hedge,
The light in huntsmen's upper story
Were parts of an eternal glory,
Were God's eternal garden flowers,
I stood in bliss at this for hours.[1]

This mind-expanding experience is similar to Pascal's ecstasy at the time of his conversion. This famous mathematician and former agnostic wrote a description of his conversion experience which was found pinned inside the lining of his coat at the time of his death. It read as follows:

"The year of grace, 1664.

. . . . From about half past ten in the evening until about half an hour after midnight,

Fire!

God of Abraham, God of Isaac, God of Jacob,

Not of the Philosophers and Savants.

Servitude! Servitude! Feeling! Joy! Peace!" [2]

Not long ago a devout Christian woman asked, "Is something wrong with me if I don't seem to get anything out of a public worship service? Sometimes nothing happens. There is no inspiration. Life seems to be just a drab plane. At other times I find real inspiration and strength."

A young person in the church, after hearing about the youth movements, such as the "Jesus Freaks" and others, asked, "Why doesn't something exciting ever happen in our church services?"

Is there a place for ecstatic experiences, for "mind-expansion"? Is it legitimate to want to break out of the mundane ordinariness of life? Why do people want this heady experience, this breaking into the bright, clean atmosphere and breathing free? How is this related to Christian experience?

Such so-called "mystical" experiences and excitement have historically had a place among religious seekers. Man has always desired to experience the ultimate, to taste the eternal dimensions that assure him there are realities beyond the earthbound levels of experience. The eighth-century prophet Isaiah saw the Lord "high and lifted up," and the Lord touched him and spoke to him. First-century Paul had an "experience that was not fitting to talk about." Many Christian pietists and mystics have written about such experiences.

The mind or spirit of man needs at times to take flights of transcendence, to walk a high road with one greater than himself.

This proves to him there are ultimate realities of life beyond the earthly bonds limited by physical and rational laws.

The ecstatic experience of God's presence refreshes and cleanses the mind and heart. This is the "total experience" many people seek. In it is fulness and a glimpse of self-realization.

Some extremists have made religious excitement the goal of their lives. Many searchers experiment with drugs to induce mind-expansion. Others seek the Oriental mysticism of "getting in touch with the universe as a whole" or "becoming absorbed with the great All." The answer to this search has been provided by God in the person of his Son Jesus Christ. By means of resurrection power he has broken all the bonds of earthly existence and death itself; he is alive to the person who seeks him by faith.

Wayne Oates suggests that the Christian cannot "deepen" his spiritual life unless he is willing to widen his perceptive capacities. He asked, "Do you practice prayer with listening to the various sounds, tones, and noises around you? Do you practice the presence of God by relaxing your whole body consciously?"

Indeed, you do not have to go to an Indian *Guru,* or wiseman, or learn this in Bombay or Calcutta. You do not have to use drugs or be hypnotized or have psychotherapy. You can begin by praying and meditating as a Christian where you are. This is one way of expanding the mind, "opening the spirit" to God.

In fact, the synthetic, man-made procedures cannot reach the inner layers of man's personality. They do not produce what they promise. Their temporary stimuli cannot sustain the confident ground on which man's real self depends. Only communion with God, the source of personal being, can provide such assurance.

There is value in having a mind-expanding experience with God. We must remember, however, that man does not live by ecstasy alone. Nowhere does the Bible imply that man was made to live always in a mystical, rarified atmosphere. No religious teacher appealed less to excitement than the founder of Christianity, Jesus Christ himself. His emphasis was placed on moral and ethical action. He was primarily concerned with the fruits of faith.

Most of life is experienced in a rather routine manner, and it is not always exciting. In fact, man could not endure such emotional excitement constantly. He acknowledges the fact of it, and in between these confrontations with God he lives by the laws and teachings of God without high ecstasy.

One danger of the psychedelic age is that we become preoccupied with our feelings. Even religious worship which gives too much attention to feelings is unhealthy. Subjectivism in prayer and singing and testimony may indicate an unstable and unhealthy condition.

God's visitation of power and grace is his gift and not our achievement. To praise him and to learn truth from him is our business. The giving of power and ecstasy is his business.

Once we have experienced God's presence, it is our privilege to live in the strength of it. In the unexciting activities and unpleasant duties we can then find a deep and confident joy. We must live by what we know and not merely by what we feel. Obedience to God's teaching brings its own joy and occasionally a mountain-top experience. Christians should neither be afraid of ecstasy nor yet rely too much upon it.

God's Word

I saw the Lord sitting upon a throne,
High and lifted up; and his
Train filled the temple. . . .
The seraphim called to each other and said,
"Holy, Holy, Holy is the Lord of Hosts,"
The whole earth is full of his glory. . . .
I heard the voice of the Lord saying,
"Whom shall I send and who will go for us?"
Then I said, "Here I am! Send me."

—Isaiah 6:1,3,8

And Jesus took with him Peter, James, and John, and brought them by themselves up to a high mountain apart from the rest. Here in their presence he was transfigured; and his clothes became glistering with a radiant whiteness, such as no bleaching on earth could give. . . . "Master," said Peter addressing Jesus, "It is good for us to be here. . . ." (for he did not know what to say, they were so awe-struck).

—Mark 9:2–3,5–6, Centenary

Do not be drunk with wine, in which there is riotous living, but drink deep in the Spirit, when you talk together; with psalms and hymns and spiritual songs, singing and with all your hearts making music unto the Lord; and at all times for all things give thanks to God, the Father, in the name of our Lord Jesus Christ.

—Ephesians 5:18–20, Centenary

A Prayer

God gives us himself that we may share him with others.

He gives us great joy that our griefs may be more bearable

He gives us his strength that we may serve his people without fainting.

He gives us visions of glory that smog in the valley may not dim our view.

He gives us his grace and acceptance that we may never feel entirely rejected.

Lord, since this is true,

Help us to be open to your visitation

And willing to do your will. Amen.

NOTES

1. Alfred C. Underwood, *Conversion: Christian and Non-Christian* (London: George Allen and Unwin, Ltd., 1925), p. 163.

2. *Ibid.*, p. 166.

5.
RING A MERRY BELL

In mid-nineteenth century Puritan England Charles Hadden Spurgeon preached a sermon on the joys of celebration. It was based on the text Job 1:4–5 which relates that the sons and daughters of Job feasted (celebrated) with joy in their houses every day, and Job dedicated them and their celebrations to God.

Spurgeon said, "As this incident was festive, so we will ring a merry bell." The preacher went on to say, "God forbid that I should be such a Puritan as to proclaim the annihilation of any day of rest (such as Christmas) which falls to the lot of the laboring man." He reminded his congregation that they should feast and rejoice, and, as God had given them substance, endeavor to make their households glad.

As there is license for feasting and celebrating, there is also caution against wrong kinds of celebration which is a sin against God. Job's sons feasted in *good houses,* in *good company,* with *good behavior,* for a *good purpose.*

The Bible tells the story of a people who rejoiced in feasts and celebrations throughout their history. The highest point of their celebration was the Feast of the Passover, kept in commemoration of their deliverance from slavery in Egypt. They gave thanks to God who delivered them.

Jesus himself attended feasts and parties where there was joy and celebration. At a wedding feast he helped provide good cheer and contributed his own efforts at making the feast a success.

On one occasion Jesus reminded his hearers of the dynamic of the good news. He warned the legalists and traditionalists, "You can't keep new wine, with its ferment, its enthusiasm, in old wineskin containers. It must have room for celebration. It must break out of the old skins, the old traditions. The Christian gospel is full of life and power."

All of us have had moments of celebration for the blessings of life. For example, when our oldest son called us at one-thirty A.M. and proudly announced the birth of our first grandson, we were filled with joy. Not only would he perpetuate the family name, but he was also to carry his grandfather's first name!

In our excitement Fannie Mae and I could not return to sleep. I said, "We must celebrate! We don't smoke cigars, and we don't drink champagne, but we have some ginger ale." So we opened the bottle of ginger ale and gave a toast to our grandson. Then we went to the piano and played and sang, "Praise God from whom all blessings flow" at two o'clock in the morning. What if we did disturb the neighbors! Who cares in a time like that?

Have you ever had something good to happen which you felt you must share? You could hardly wait to tell the good news to your friends.

God wants us to live our lives in joy and thanksgiving. The gospel is good news to be celebrated. The Christian life is not a routine of rules and regulations to be followed so much as it is an experience to be lived. It should be lived with enthusiasm.

There are numerous times in our lives when we should ring a merry bell in celebration. One's conversion is such an experience. As Underwood said, "There runs through the New Testament writings strong tides of religious life and emotion. The early church was a church of converted men and women. They speak as converts, they write as converts, and they exult as converts."

Ring a merry bell at a wedding. When two young people commit themselves in marriage they may well give thanks to God for promise of a happy life together. In the Middle East it is still the custom for the whole community to join in a processional to the groom's house and to congratulate him. Traveling in Jordan a few years ago, we encountered such a group who slowly parted in the street to let us pass. They were celebrating wildly.

Ring a merry bell at the birth of a new baby. The first thought of Christian parents is to give thanks to God for their privilege of caring for a new life. Jesus' parents took him to the Temple for dedication soon after his birth.

Ring a merry bell when a child in the family is promoted from one grade to another, when he graduates from high school, and when he receives his college diploma.

Ring a merry bell upon moving into a new home. When one's dreams of many years have come to fruition, it is a time to give thanks to God. The old custom of having a "housewarming" and helping a couple furnish a new home can be a meaningful experience for an entire community.

Ring a merry bell when a peace armistice has been signed. At the end of World War II a day was set aside as V-J Day in the churches. God's people, many of whom had lost members of their families in the war, gave thanks to God for peace again in our time.

Ring a merry bell upon recovering from illness. Health and healing are a blessing of God.

Ring a merry bell at public worship in the church. Worship should be seen as a privilege to be enjoyed, and not merely a duty to be performed.

David Head raises the question,

I wonder how much of a "kick" we get out of worship these days. Some preachers have voices like funeral bells, some congregations like pagan funeral dirges. The writer of Psalm 122 said he was *glad* when they said to him "Let us go into the house of the Lord." The worship of God in heaven must be a complete enjoyment, and we are meant to share in that enjoyment in our worship on earth. Surely reverence and joy belong together in Christian worship! [1]

God's Word

Bless the Lord, O my soul;
And all that is within me,
Bless his holy name!
Bless the Lord, O my soul,
And forget not all his benefits,
Who forgives all your iniquity,
Who heals all your diseases,
Who redeems your life from the Pit,
Who crowns you with steadfast love and mercy,
Who satisfies you with good as long as you live
So that your youth is renewed like the eagle's.

—Psalm 103:1–5

Praise the Lord!
O give thanks to the Lord,
For he is good;
For his steadfast love endures forever!

—Psalm 106:1

Whatever you do, in word or deed, do everything in the name of the Lord Jesus, giving thanks to God the Father through him.

—Colossians 3:17

A Prayer

This is the day which thou hast made, O Lord.
Let us rejoice and be glad in it!
Let us be glad for life that it may be full rather than empty.
Let us be glad for family, for by it life is enriched.
Let us be glad for health, for many never find it.
Let us be glad for work, for by it our hands produce.

Let us be glad for church, for our lives are completed in others. Let us be Glad! Amen.

NOTES

1. David Head, *Countdown: The Launching of Prayer in the Space Age* (New York: Macmillan Co., 1963), p. 12.

6.
GOD IS ALWAYS THERE

On a sharecropper farm, hidden back in the woods at the foot of a "mountain range"—a small boy's term for Oklahoma hill country—one evening our cows failed to come home at milking time.

As my father prepared to go look for them, he asked me if I wanted to join him. What seven-year-old boy would not like to go with his dad anywhere! He lighted a lantern and off we went!

As we entered the woods the darkness grew deeper. Suddenly Father blew out the lantern light and disappeared. For an instant I was afraid, but only for an instant. I thought, "I don't know where my father is, but I know him and he will allow no harm to come to me." I relaxed and waited. In a moment he stepped from behind a tree, laughing and teasing me. Then he lighted the lantern, and we were on our way.

Even now, in these lengthening years of life, I look around, and God the heavenly Father sometimes seems to be absent. He withholds or hides himself. It is a frightening experience to feel that God is absent and that you are alone.

John Henry Newman once observed that what is so painful in

life is God's seeming absence from his own universe. And yet, Newman really knew better from experience, for he also wrote,

> Lead kindly light! Amid th' encircling gloom,
> Lead thou me on;
> The night is dark, and I am far from home,
> Lead thou me on;
> Keep thou my feet; I do not ask to see
> The distant scene; One step enough for me.

Of course, God is not really absent. In our limited ability to experience him, he only seems to be. He is not an absentee God. He did not create the world and its inhabitants and then leave it to run itself.

The world-famed scientist-priest Pierre Theilhard de Chardin, in *Hymn of the Universe* expressed it thus:

> As for us creatures,
> Of ourselves we are but emptiness and obscurity.
> But you, my God, are the inmost depths,
> The stability of that eternal *milieu,*
> Without duration or space,
> In which our cosmos emerges gradually into being
> And grows gradually to its final completeness,
> As it loses those boundaries
> Which to our eyes seem so immense.[1]

As all-wise, eternal Creator, God has both the ability and the right to hide himself or withhold himself from us. He does not always have to be demonstrative. He has revealed enough for us to rely on.

God's presence is dynamic and personal, not merely mechanical or spatial. He controls physical laws, but he is not mere physical law.

As supreme person he is free to respond to us and to grant our requests. He is not an unbending tyrant. What he does is not arbitrary.

God is purposeful. He sees the end from the beginning in our lives. Therefore, what he does makes sense.

God is close and warm as our Father. Jesus revealed a new dimension in God. The Old Testament speaks of God as Creator, as sovereign Lord, as one who provides, and as all-wise. Jesus speaks of him as Father.

As Father, God is aware of us.

As Father, he is sensitive to our needs.

As Father, he stands by to protect us.

As Father, he has the resources to provide for us.

As Father, he responds to our cry when we hurt.

As Father, he walks ahead of us in the pathway.

As Father, in love he forgives us.

As Father, through Christ he redeems us by his grace.

As Father, he is always present in his Spirit.

As Father, he disciplines us firmly when we stray.

When Alexander MacLaren, the Bible expositor, was sixteen years old, he got his first job in the city of Glasgow. As he left for Glasgow his father said, "Alex, we'll be looking for you Saturday night after the week's work is over. Come home so that we can go to the church together on next Lord's Day."

As the time drew near for his return home on that Saturday night, Alex remembered that robbers sometimes waylaid people on the rugged road at night, and he was afraid. As he neared a deep, dark gulch, where thugs could be hiding, he stopped and hesitated. In a moment he saw a figure rise up in the path out of the darkness. Soon he recognized his father who had come to meet him, for he knew Alex would be afraid. Arm in arm father and son walked down the dark road together on their way home where the family worshiped God on the Lord's Day.

God's Word

The God who made the world and everything in it. . . . is not far from each one of us, for "In him we live and move and have our being."

—Acts 17:24,27–28

It is the Lord that goes before you; he will be with you and he will not fail you or forsake you; do not fear or be dismayed.

—Deuteronomy 31:8

I will pray the Father, and he will give you another Counselor, to be with you for ever, even the Spirit of truth . . . you know him, for he dwells with you, and will be in you. I will not leave you desolate; I will come to you.

—John 14:16–18

A Prayer Hymn

He leadeth me! O blessed tho't!
O words with heavenly comfort fraught!
Whate'er I do, Where'er I be,
Still 'tis God's hand that leadeth me!

Sometimes 'mid scenes of deepest gloom,
Sometimes where Eden's bowers bloom,
By waters still, o'er troubled sea
Still 'tis God's hand that leadeth me!

Lord, I would clasp my hand in thine,
Nor ever murmur nor repine;
Content, whatever lot I see,
Since 'tis thy hand that leadeth me!

He leadeth me, He leadeth me,
By His own hand He leadeth me:
His faithful follower I would be,
For by His hand he leadeth me. Amen.

NOTES

1. Pierre Teilhard de Chardin, *Hymn of the Universe* (New York: Harper and Row, 1965), p. 21 f.

7.
WHAT! ME A SAINT?

"Nobody is perfect!" This old adage is often an excuse for being less than we are supposed to be. The idea of perfection can be a challenge or a handicap, depending upon one's interpretation of it.

The "perfectionist syndrome" is life's greatest obstacle for some people. It can be a threat to the enjoyment of life and even to life's accomplishments. One's frustrations and obsessions with his faults and failures may be due to his false concept of perfection as a goal for man.

When God said, "Be ye holy, for I am holy," he was not setting forth an ethical rule of perfection for man. Rather, he was speaking of total commitment of life to the purposes and glory of God.

Stephen Neill says that the biblical concept of holiness is always a religious and not primarily an ethical idea. God alone is holy. The term "holy" means set apart or dedicated to a given purpose.

Holiness has primarily to do with the object of one's worship. Man is to be holy, set apart unto God and his purposes. Only as man becomes aware of God does he become aware also of the dimensions of holiness.

The Bible speaks of Israel as God's chosen and separated or holy people. They were holy because they were separated unto God. The same truth runs through the New Testament concerning those who are called of God and who respond to him by faith in Christ.

The perfectionist makes too great a demand upon himself. He sets his goals beyond reasonable expectations and then strains to reach them, stretching sometimes to the breaking point.

The opposite effect of a false view of perfection may be that a person will give up striving because he knows he can't be perfect. He becomes self-satisfied or lethargic. He becomes morally lazy.

Ethical or moral righteousness is not a state of private and inner consecration. It is primarily a matter of relationships—to God who made and redeemed man and to all other men.

Rudolph Otto emphasized the majesty and transcendence of God as the foundation to religious experience. The sense of awe which he called the *"Mysterium Tremendum"* motivates man to ethical and moral behavior. Our hope for holiness, wholeness, commitment, perfection, is to be found in Christ.

We share in the factors always present in the holiness of Jesus: 1) realism, an understanding of the realities of a given situation; 2) austerity, even a stern demand for growth toward maturity; 3) compassion, a sympathy that serves to spur to redemptive action; 4) patience, that gives time for transformation to take effect; 5) hope, a faith anchored in the faithfulness of God to bring his people to maturity.[1]

There is a place for discipline and self-discipline in the Christian life. The Christian is committed to keeping God's commandments, to performing life's tasks which include the routine activities. He has moments of inspiration, visions of God's holiness. These experiences give him the strength to persist in the business of living day by day.

A newspaper columnist wrote an article on "Practical Perfection Possible." He says that Jesus was aware of human frailty and was not talking about ethical perfection when he said, "Be thou perfect." He actually means "get yourself together," or "dedicate yourself to one supreme purpose." He says that it is a practical rather than a utopian task.

When Will Rogers was asked, "What's wrong with the world?" he said, "Well, I don't know. I guess its people." Man must acknowledge his sin, his brokeness, his alienation.

A recent writer said, "Every man's civil war throws him into competition and conflict with his fellows, and they with him." The Fall in Genesis was man's fall into bondage to his own conflicting instincts, hungers, and aspirations. Before man can ever mature and grow toward perfection he must get his directions straight. Perfectionism roots in self-interest. It is "kissin' cousin" to self-righteousness.[2] To aim at being God is a sin of the inner self. To play at being God is the sin of relationships.

If we grow toward perfection it will be out of the grace and strength of our fellowship in Christ. He is our righteousness. We should not be preoccupied with our own state of goodness. Rather, let us concentrate upon *doing* the truth, on fulfilling God's command concerning our daily conduct.

When our minds are focused on our relationship to God and our faithfulness on his commands, our maturity will follow naturally.

God's Word
Holy, Holy, Holy is the Lord of hosts; the whole earth is full of his glory.
—Isaiah 6:3

May the God of peace himself sanctify you wholly; and may your spirit and soul and body be kept sound and blameless at the coming of our Lord Jesus Christ. He who calls you is faithful, and he will do it.

—1 Thessalonians 5:23–24

I do not consider myself to have "arrived," spiritually, nor do I consider myself already perfect. But I keep going on, grasping ever more firmly that purpose for which Christ Jesus grasped me. My brothers, I do not consider myself to have fully grasped it even now.

But I do concentrate on this: I leave the past behind and with my hands outstretched to whatever lies ahead I go straight for the goal—my reward the honor of my high calling by God in Christ Jesus.

—Philippians 3:12–14, Phillips

A Prayer

Sometimes I try to play a game—
I pretend I can reach perfection
But I know that is not possible.
Only you are truly perfect, O God.
Give me the grace to accept my humanity
Give me the desire to become more like Christ
Help me to grow in grace and knowledge
That my life may be more mature
And my daily deeds more useful.

Amen.

NOTES

1. Stephen Neill, *Christian Holiness* (New York: Harper and Bros., 1960), p. 22.
2. Wallace E. Fisher, *Can Man Hope to Be Human?* (Nashville: Abingdon Press, 1971), p. 21.

8.
ON FINDING THE RIGHT KEY

The author of *Alice in Wonderland,* Lewis Carroll, wrote a story entitled "The Lock." It told about a lock running here and there all over the place. When asked why it was rushing around so, the lock answered, "You see, I'm locked up tight, and I'm searching for a key that will unlock me."

The businessman with more responsibility than he can handle, or perhaps with frustrations over the ethical thing to do in the competitive business world, needs a key that will unlock his anxieties. In this tension between the ideal and the practical, what is this key?

A young man is entering the college classroom. For the first time he is confronted with intellectual doubt as he encounters new areas of knowledge. "What is truth?" keeps resounding in his ears. He must find the key in his search for self-identity in a world of exploding knowledge.

Mrs. Housewife, shut up with her housekeeping, feels that she is forgotten. Does she have any real worth? Does anyone really care about her? The drudgery of the routine of housewifery is really getting to her. Surely there is a key that will unlock this prison of her soul.

The pastor of the old First Church talks so much he gets bored with all that repetition. As he reads the Bible over and over again, there sets in a sort of "deadening familiarity with the sublime," as J. H. Jowett wrote in his classic *The Preacher, His Life and His Work*. Is there a key to unlock the pastor's dilemma?

The proper key may be a brief period of prayer each day. A school administrator found this to be his key. He was chairman of deacons in his church. The church asked him to serve as chairman of the building fund campaign so they could proceed with the building of their new sanctuary.

During that year, when he felt the load was too heavy, he would often enter his office and tell the secretary he was not to be disturbed for fifteen minutes. Closing the door, he would bow his head on the desk, relax, and talk with God. Always he found "renewed strength and courage."

A working man who had always tried to be honest thought he was "a pretty good fellow." He attended a revival meeting where he heard a plain sermon on sin and the need for salvation in Christ. He said, "I began to see myself a sinner. My own self-righteousness was not enough. I felt God pushing me down the aisle to confess my sins and to accept Christ. After that experience I felt good about my relationship to God." The key to his problem was the grace of God in Christ.

Bishop Canon Charles Gore of England once prepared to preach an Easter sermon. He wrestled in prayer to find the inspiration he needed. He found the key to the routineness of his Christian experience. That Sunday when he stood to preach he said, "I know Jesus Christ is alive, because I talked with him this morning." The reality of the resurrection was the key that unlocked the pastor's ability to preach with power.

You see, you and I must search for the right key. We must be responsible for our lives. If we give up the search, we become irresponsible. We are already dead, even though we are still breathing. There is always a key for the spirit. God's key ring is unlimited.

These keys God has provided:
The love of family
The fellowship of the church
Spacious skies and amber fields of grain
A world of exploding knowledge
Sharp minds of gifted teachers
A library called the Bible—
These keys will unlock you and me.
Reach out—
And take a key
Unlock yourself
Be open to God
Be open to other persons
Be open to your vocation
Be open with yourself
For growth
For ministry
For the enjoyment of life.

God's Word

I do not understand what I do; for I don't do what I would like to do, but instead I do what I hate. . . . what an unhappy man I am! Who will rescue me from this body that is taking me to death? Thanks be to God through our Lord Jesus Christ!

—Romans 7:15,24–25, TEV[1]

If any of you lacks wisdom he should pray to God, who will give it to you; for God gives generously and graciously to all. But you must believe when you pray and not doubt at all; for whoever doubts is like a wave of the sea that is driven and blown about by the wind.

—James 1:5–6, TEV

The Lord is near; have no anxiety, but in everything make your requests known to God in prayer and petition with thanksgiving. Then the peace of God, which is beyond our utmost understanding, will keep guard over your hearts and your thoughts, in Christ Jesus.

—Philippians 4:6–7, NEB[2]

A Prayer

God of all resources,
Help me find the right key to unlock myself
Give me the courage to take the key in hand
Move in my spirit to turn the key with firmness
Give me wisdom to enter the doors
Which your key opens up to me
In Christ's name. Amen.

NOTES

1. From the Today's English Version of the New Testament. Copyright American Bible Society 1966. All succeeding quotations from this version are indicated by the abbreviation TEV in parentheses.

2. From the New English Bible, New Testament, Second Edition. © The Delegates of the Oxford University Press, and the Syndics of the Cambridge University Press 1961, 1970. Reprinted by permission. All succeeding quotations from this version are indicated by the abbreviation NEB in parentheses.

9.
TIME FOR LIVING

People who knew Justice Louis D. Brandeis recognized that he was a tireless worker. However, he believed in taking periodic vacations. He was convinced that these intervals of relaxation made it possible for him to increase his work load.

A colleague once chided him for going on a trip when he had an important trial coming up. Brandeis explained, "I need this period of change. I can do a year's work in eleven months, but not in twelve."

How often you have heard people say, "I wish I had time to do the things I have always wanted to do." America has entered the period when people will have more time for selected living. More "nonwork" time will be available.

For people who have been accustomed to the forty-hour work week or more, it is difficult to imagine the four-day work week. Many businesses are already experimenting with this schedule.

Always there are the "unemployed" who would like to work if they could find a job. The percentage of unemployed in America varies from time to time. These persons are faced with the meaningful use of time.

Physically handicapped people, unable to find a job, have agonized over the problem of time-use for years. Many of them have learned to do creative work and to make good use of their time.

The elderly "retiree" is faced with more time available than he has known during his working years. In a White House Conference on Aging, Dr. Max Kaplan, Director for the Center of Studies on Leisure, the University of Florida, Tampa, described the needs and wants of the aging as "changing life-styles and commitments."

In another category is the nonworker by choice. He is living off "accumulated wealth" and is not tied down to a traditional job. One such man in his early forties rejects the idea that a man must "work" for a living in the traditional sense. For years he has engaged in the creative arts, in the study of sociological problems, and in politics and public service.

American citizens have traditionally felt that long hours of physical labor is the ideal way to prove that life has meaning. The "Protestant work ethic" has produced guilt feelings concerning leisure time. This philosophy has accelerated with the coming of "mass production." It is interesting that in the land where Christianity began, the people have historically been more leisure-loving. They live at a slower pace and feel this is according to the will of God.

Dr. Kaplan suggests that most workers do not get satisfaction from the mechanics of their job but from the "self view" in the eyes of colleagues and from the human relationships on the job. He feels that we need to move into meaningful nonwork roles. He calls for new forms of commitment in which "skills are useful, human relationships are crucial, and the dignity that comes from being needed is supported.

People who take life seriously always find time a problem. In the fourth century Augustine described his own difficulty with relating time to work and leisure:

For what is time? Who can easily and briefly explain it?. . . . if no one asks of me, I know; if I wish to explain it to him who asks, I know not.

In one of Henry Bergson's writings, life is likened to a clock which has been wound up and is ticking off the minutes, until it comes to its inevitable end—which is death.

Lee suggests there are various ways of looking at time, all of which affect our understanding of the meaning of life. There is the cyclical view of time which recurs with the constant succession of night and day.

With the new forms that accompany scientific and economic developments time is seen as progression.

The primary way of regarding time in our culture is in terms of "clock time." We get up, work, eat, sleep, play, visit, and, in short, live by what time the clock tells us it is.

Men in the technological age reckon time as money. Adam Smith observed that work produces goods and goods produce wealth.

Time is also seen in a social sense. Quantitative units of time are used to produce commodities people need.

To the Christian time is seen as God's creation. It is his gift to man for opportunity and fulfilment. The Bible has two primary words for time, *chronos,* the temporal succession of time, and *kairos,* the time of God's appointments and man's opportunity.

Time is man's opportunity for freedom to be exercised. Only when there is commitment can God-given freedom be fulfilled. No time is free of normative constraints.

Perhaps the following forms of time-use can be helpful to us in making life more meaningful and self-fulfilling:

Stopping by a clean, flowing brook. Remember Robert Frost's "Stopping by a Wood on a Snowy Day."

Reading what one enjoys reading—a poem, a bit of fiction, a devotional essay, or a mind-expanding treatise. In their book *A*

Window on the Mountain Winston and Winnie Pearce suggest ways to "cut windows" by reading which opens up the horizon to beauty, truth, and purpose.

Solitude provides time for meditation. Since the days of Thoreau's *Walden* men have been challenged to invest some time in solitude.

Entertainment—that means of enjoying the talents which other people share out of their treasure of creativity.

Sports and other physical activity, such as fishing, golf, etc., often bring vigor into life.

Hobbies often fill life to the brim, especially if one has developed meaningful activities through the years: ceramics, painting, bird-watching, "rock-hounding," and others.

Sharing life with convalescents through visiting, witnessing, and dialogue can be enriching.

The fine art of listening takes time, more time than most of us are willing to give.

Robert Browning had Rabbi Ben Ezra exclaim,

Grow old along with me!
The best is yet to be
The last of life, for which the first was made.
Our times are in His hand.

God's Word
Our years come to an end like a sigh.
The years of our life are threescore and ten,
Or even by reason of strength fourscore;
Yet their span is but toil and trouble;
They are soon gone, and we fly away.
So teach us to number our days
That we may get a heart of wisdom.

—Psalm 90:9b–10,12

For everything there is a season,
And a time for every matter under heaven:

A time to be born, and a time to die;
A time to plant, and a time to pluck up what is planted;
A time to kill, and a time to heal;
A time to break down, and a time to build up,
A time to weep, and a time to laugh;
A time to mourn, and a time to dance;
A time to cast away stones, and a time to gather stones
  together;
A time to embrace, and a time to refrain from embracing;
A time to seek, and a time to lose;
A time to keep, and a time to cast away;
A time to rend, and a time to sew;
A time to keep silence, and a time to speak;
A time to love, and a time to hate;
A time for war, and a time for peace.

—Ecclesiastes 3:1–8

Look carefully then how you walk, not as unwise men but as wise, making the most of the time, because the days are evil.

—Ephesians 5:15–16

A Prayer

Lord, I have time,
I have plenty of time,
All the time that you give me,
The years of my life,
The days of my years,
The hours of my days,
They are all mine.
Mine to fill, quietly, calmly,
But to fill completely, up to the brim,
To offer them to you, that of their insipid water
You may make a rich wine
Such as you made once in Cana of Galilee.
I am not asking you tonight, Lord,
For time to do this and then that,
But your grace to do conscientiously in the time

That you give me,
What you want me to do.[1] Amen.

NOTES

1. Michel Quoist, *Prayers* (New York: Sheed and Ward, Inc., 1963).

10.
FORGIVEN AND FORGIVING

When ancient Judah had sinned against God, Jeremiah was deeply burdened for their guilt. He prayed:

My grief is beyond healing,
My heart is sick within me.
Is there no balm in Gilead?
Is there no physican there?
Why then has the health of the daughter
Of my people not been restored?
O that my head were waters,
And my eyes a fountain of tears,
That I might weep day and night,
For the slain of the daughter of my people!

—Jeremiah 8:18,22; 9:1

Are you a sinner? Do you ever do wrong and need forgiveness? I confess that I do.

When we speak of "sins" we usually list gross iniquities—lustful sensuality, robbery, drunkenness, murder, and the like. Then we seek to exempt ourselves from the company of sinners.

A prominent pastor-preacher said that before any person endeavors to avoid his share in the need of forgiveness he should add at least three categories to the above list of sins.[1] The first would be *the sins of temperament*—sullenness, vindictiveness, peevishness, jealousy, bad temper.

A second list are *sins of social attitude,* such as love of money, racial prejudice, economic injustice, political irresponsibility.

Then all of us need forgiveness for *sins of neglect*—words we fail to speak, deeds we never perform, acts of mercy we forgot to carry out, neglected opportunities.

One of my greatest needs is sensitivity and awareness of my own sins. A fellow-minister Daniel Walker spoke to me in his book *The Human Problems of the Minister.* In a chapter "Condemned to Sin Piously," he warns against pretense as a vocational hazard for ministers. Perhaps other Christians also need this warning.

No one can enumerate all his sins. Indeed, only God's mercy is wider than our guilt. Walker says,

> Think of the fears we are ashamed to admit, our failure to come to terms with sex, our personal animosities, our careless handling of finances, our lack of faith, our thin devotional life, our strained family relations, our weaknesses as pastors, our impatience and our selfish ambitions, to name only a few of our shortcomings.[2]

Someone said of Gladstone that his tendency was to believe that his desires were those of the Almighty. All of us are tempted to claim divine sanction for behavior more "congenial to the devil."

Because sin is serious, forgiveness is difficult. It is even difficult for God. That is, God cannot easily overlook our sins. The gospel is not a sentimental offer of "cheap grace," as Bonhoeffer said in *The Cost of Discipleship.* To condone sin is easy; to forgive sin is hard.

Forgiveness cost God the death of his Son. The cross was the price of grace. Because Jesus himself knew the seriousness of sin, as he offered forgiveness, he said, "Go thy way and sin no more."

Love does not forgive at a shallow level. It is not sentimental.

When one is wronged by a person he loves, he finds it difficult to forgive because he feels the hurt so deeply. In fact, he shares the guilt of the one he loves.

In the sentimental best-selling novel *Love Story* the outstanding theme is expressed in the song "Love Means Never Having to Say You're Sorry." On the surface it sounds beautiful, but it is a shallow concept of love. In our sinful human milieu we often have to say, "I'm sorry" to those we genuinely love.

Dr. Fosdick reminded us that forgiveness is a soul-shaking experience for the one forgiven. Forgiveness does not take away the fact of sin. The prodigal son had indeed been in a "far country."

Forgiveness does not take away the memory of sin. The prodigal will never forget what he has done. Being forgiven does help him to live with the memory.

Nor can forgiveness take away all the consequences of sin. The scars still remain. The influence on other persons still goes on multiplying.

Does forgiveness have no real meaning, no real effect? Oh, yes, it does. It is dynamic and healing!

Forgiveness reestablishes the personal relationships broken by sin. The repenting sinner is brought into fellowship with God. He is now a man in Christ. Forgiveness makes the relationship deeper and sweeter because grace and love awaken a responsive gratitude.

God offers forgiveness to sinners! This is the heart of the gospel. The only answer to sin is repentance and confession. This is the door to forgiveness.

God's forgiveness is made possible by faith. Man accepts God's offer by opening his life to God, not running away from him, nor resisting him.

The prodigal son "came to himself." Then he said, "I will arise and go to my father and will say, 'I have sinned and am not worthy to be called your son.' "

The climax of the story came when the father ran down the road to meet his son and to assure him of his forgiveness!

There was a joyous celebration made possible by confession and forgiveness—a celebration of love at its deepest and best level.

God's Word

Blessed is he whose transgression is forgiven,
Whose sin is covered.
When I declared not my sin,
My body wasted away
Through my groaning all day long.
For day and night thy hand was
Heavy upon me;
My strength was dried up as by
The heat of summer.
I acknowledged my sin to thee,
And I did not hide my iniquity;
I said, "I will confess my transgressions to the Lord";
Then thou didst forgive the guilt of my sin.

—Psalm 32:1,3–5

Create in me a clean heart, O God,
And put a new and right spirit within me.
Cast me not away from thy presence, and
Take not thy Holy Spirit from me.
Restore to me the joy of thy salvation,
And uphold me with a willing spirit.

Psalm 51:10–12

If we confess our sins, he is faithful and just, and will forgive our sins and cleanse us from all unrighteousness.

—1 John 1:9

A Prayer

My failure to be true even to my own accepted standards:
My self-deception in the face of temptation:
My choosing of the worse when I know the better:
O Lord, Forgive.

My failure to apply myself to the standards of conduct
  I demand of others:
My blindness to the suffering of others and my slowness
  to be taught by my own:
My complacence towards wrongs that do not touch
My own case and my over-sensitiveness to those that do:
My slowness to see the good in my fellows
And to see the evil in myself:
My hardness of heart toward my neighbors' faults
And my readiness to make allowance for my own:
My unwillingness to believe that thou hast called me
To a small work and my brother to a great one:
  O Lord, Forgive. Amen.[3]

NOTES

NOTES

1. H. E. Fosdick, "The Forgiveness of Sins," *The Secret of Victorious Living* (New York: Harper and Bros., 1934), pp. 110 ff.

2. Daniel Walker, *The Human Problems of the Minister* (New York: Harper and Bros., 1960), p. 2.

3. John Baillie, *A Diary of Private Prayer* (London: Oxford University Press, 1949), p. 15.

11.
THE LORD'S SUPPER: COMMAND PERFORMANCE!

The Lord's Supper is a "now" experience. After these many years of taking the bread and the cup, I recently had a new meaningful worship experience.

The bread had been passed to us in the congregation. I held the broken piece between my fingers, meditating on its meaning.

Feeling the throb of my own pulsebeat against the bread, I imagined the bread was alive. I could not distinguish between my own flesh and the piece of bread representing the body of Jesus Christ. Where does one stop and the other begin?

I thought, this is what God would have us feel in the act of worship. Christ really is present here as he is present anywhere else, and the bread reminds us of this fact.

As I ate the bread, I thought, through faith we partake of the living Christ in personal relationship just as really as I am taking this bread into my physical body.

Then I took the small glass cup of red wine (grape juice) and held it carefully with the fingers of both hands. I looked into the red liquid and saw light reflected in it. Again, with each pulsebeat the wine moved and a flame of light seemed to rise from the cup with every heartbeat.

I mused, in this act of worship the life blood of Jesus Christ responds to my prayer of faith, and the life of God gives me new spiritual strength.

How many times have you and I participated in the Lord's Supper in a merely perfunctory manner! Do we simply observe it as a ritual? Is it a mere ordinance to be obeyed as a sort of legalism?

It was given to us as God's revelation of truth, his visible word to be acted out, just as his written word is to be read and preached.

The Lord's Supper is truly meant to be an act of worship. It is more than *mere* symbolism. It is God's word made alive by the good news of the living Christ to those who open their hearts by faith to receive him.

When Jesus said, "This do in remembrance of me," he used the Greek word *anamnesis* which means "to remind" or "to recall." Actually, the act of eating the bread and drinking the wine was meant to bring to their present consciousness Christ's giving of himself to his people. The emphasis is on his presence rather than on his absence.

My first experience of participating in the Lord's Supper followed soon after I became a Christian at eleven years of age. In our little country church the pastor usually preached until after twelve o'clock. Then he and the deacons prepared to administer the Lord's Supper.

I did not really worship in this ritual. I felt it was sort of "tacked on" to the end of an already long worship service. It was years later that I began to feel the Lord's Supper should be given the central place in worship. As a perfunctory ritual it is a dull routine. As an act of worship it is a dynamic and inspiring experience.

In the presence of Christ one becomes aware of his need for confession of sins. Always his holy presence inspires humility and repentance. This act of worship brings a cleansing experience.

It climaxes in commitment. A feeling without a decision for

commitment is not genuine worship. Only personal self-giving is true worship.

The Lord's Supper is an act of the church, not a mere private experience. The individual is part of the congregation, the people of God. The church is commissioned to preach the gospel; the Lord's Supper is one way of proclaiming it.

Fellowship is experienced in the Lord's Supper. Jesus said, "Take and divide it among yourselves." Then he said of the wine, "All of you drink of it." It is a communion, a participation, an act of community.

Communion demands acceptance and love which can come only with forgiveness. We have fellowship with Christ only when we are in fellowship with one another.

The Lord's Supper is a celebration, a proclamation of the Good News. The earliest term used to designate this act of worship was Eucharist which comes from the Greek word Jesus used, *eucharisteo,* "to give thanks."

This dramatic ritual of worship also has missionary significance. In other words, "The Lord's Supper is the great preacher of the death of Christ till his second coming," as Professor A. T. Robertson said.[1]

Bishop John A. T. Robinson of England says that the Lord's Supper is "Christ's command performance." [2] Christ commanded his church to come together regularly for worship. As often as we do it, we "proclaim his death."

Our selves are made whole in the renewal which worship in the Lord's Supper brings to us in the church. In Christ we mutually find one another as his body of believers. The renewal of love comes in the act of worship.

God's Word

The Lord Jesus on the night when he was betrayed took bread, and when he had given thanks, he broke it, and said, "This is my body which is for you. Do this in remembrance of me." In the same way also the cup, after supper, saying, "This cup is the new covenant in

my blood. Do this, as often as you drink it, in remembrance of me."
For as often as you eat this bread and drink the cup, you proclaim the
Lord's death until he comes.

—1 Corinthians 11:23–26

Jesus asked, "Are you able to drink the cup I am about to drink?"
They said to him, "We are able." Jesus said, "Whoever would be great
among you must be your servant, and whoever would be first among
you must be your slave; even as the Son of man came not to be served
but to serve, and to give his life as a ransom for many."

—Matthew 20:22,26–28

With eyes wide open to the mercies of God, I beg you, my brothers,
as an act of intelligent worship, to give him your bodies, as a living
sacrifice, consecrated to him and acceptable by him.

—Romans 12:1, Phillips

A Prayer

Lord, in this act of worship
Let us identify with you:
In this exercise of faith and trust,
In humility and repentance,
Confessing every sin in our conscience,
Accepting your love and forgiveness,
Forgiving our fellow-worshippers
Of even the most despicable faults,
Committing our lives in service,
Even to the point of suffering and sacrifice,
And thus find fresh motivation
And new strength
To be your servants indeed.

Amen.

NOTES

1. A. T. Robertson, *Word Pictures of the New Testament* (New York:
Harper and Bros., 1931), Vol. 4, p. 165.
2. Bishop A. T. Robinson, *Liturgy Coming to Life* (Philadelphia: Westminster Press, 1960), p. 55.

12.
ALL THINGS ARE YOURS

Jean Holzhauer says:

"Modern times have done all right by me and mine, and I'm grateful for every gram of Salk vaccine, penicillin, tetanus serum, antibiotics, and aspirin; every box of detergent and jet-propelled cereal; for all vitamin capsules, cancer research, telephone service, indoor plumbing, pure-food-and-drug laws, fair-employment legislation, voting franchises, social security, and exploration of the outer space available. I am a long way from regarding this as the best of all possible worlds, but neither can I bring myself to think of it as irredeemable squalor which Christians must reject to secure their own salvation. My faith in a just and loving God is strengthened by the secular wonders he has permitted his children to achieve." [1]

In a current magazine a sociologist declared, "A new God is needed for the space age." According to this writer, religion is outmoded, and man must create his own gods.

Of course, he is speaking only from his own experience. With all his knowledge of the world of space, he is limited in his understanding of the life order. He sees only one side of man's experience—the sensory.

Some Christians make as great error by claiming only the so-called "spiritual" area of life. They tend to separate the secular from the sacred.

In the first instance man is too much involved in the material world. He is earthbound having no sense of the eternal.

The second man is just as limited as he detaches himself from the real world in which he lives. He is romanticist and other-worldly.

Paul was a realist. He declared, "All things are yours, whether the world of persons, the world of things, or the eternal order of life and death and God himself." He also is speaking from experience—what he knows.

Man has always had his problems in relation to the mysteries of the universe. He sometimes give an overemphasis to man and exalts him to a high pedestal. At other times he builds fences around man so that he cannot reach out to his full potential.

There are always two classes of worldly-wise men—the men of affairs in material things, and the philosophers who dote on the intellectual. We should never put our trust in man as the ultimate.

The Christian should never claim either too little or too much. Most of us claim too little. The Christian life is meant to be a veritable treasure. It is full and abundant.

As you look about you, claim all things for Christ. You belong to Christ, and Christ is God's Son. Therefore, you have inherited all things from him.

Claim the material realm. Material things are not evil in themselves. The psalmist exclaimed, "Bless the Lord O my soul, and forget not all his benefits!" In his enumeration of these blessings he included food, clothing and shelter, and all other material things.

The beauty of the earth is yours and mine. I have a wealthy neighbor who lives on the other side of the stream. He keeps his property like a park, with shrubs and flowers, and even geese and swans swimming gracefully on the water. It is all mine to enjoy.

What wealth can match the golden rays of the sun, or the silver beams of the moon, or the copper of the burnished storm cloud, or the multi-colored glory of the autumnal forest? What music can surpass the lilting trill of the lark or the creative melody of the mockingbird, or the mournful booming of the sea waves? All these are yours!

The English novelist, Richard Jeffries, in his fight with a cruel disease, found comfort in the wild life round him. He said, "Every blade of grass was mine, and the wild hawk circling overhead and the lark making love to his mate. Oh, happy, happy days! So beautiful to watch; and all mine!"

There are new frontiers to be claimed in the realm of scientific advancement and invention—biochemistry and our food supply, electronics and communications, miracle drugs and health, high energy physics and space travel.

All things are yours in the personal realm, the world of persons. A professor of biochemistry at Texas University challenged and inspired me with his book *You Are Extraordinary.* He wrote "Statistical man has little to do with you or me or any other real person." People are as distinctive as marbles—glass, agate, plastic, steel, multi-colored, striped, mottled. There is no such thing as "average" man. Each has his own individual worth.

God made only one you and only one me. He did not mean for us to conform to a mold. You have a particular appearance, a special ability, a distinct task at which you work creatively. No one performs exactly as you do.

But we are more than individuals. We are a part of a society of persons—family heritage, with all the deposits and memories; friends and neighbors—my first teacher in public school, the college professor who shared a cultural dimension as well as a knowledge of French; a deacon who shared his wisdom with a young preacher; the black woman servant who loved our children and who with her own hands beat out the fire blazing on the clothing of one of our little boys. Now she calls herself second grandmother to his own little girl.

All things are yours in the spiritual realm, the realm of faith: personal redemption in Christ. The grace of God has united us with Christ as Savior and planted his own life dynamic within us as deep as life itself.

A fellowship of believers in the church is yours. The same Spirit dwells in all God's people, and we are conscious of a unity of persons. We are truly one body.

Even Christ himself is yours. That is, he lives in you and makes his life available to you every moment of your days. He said, "I am the vine, you are the branches. Abide in me, and I in you. As the Father has loved me, so have I loved you; abide in my love" (see John 15). What a privilege to have the life of Christ available to each one of us!

The climax to our claim is that we belong to Christ. He has claimed us, chosen us, cleansed us, adopted us into his kingdom.

We are not our own. We are his loved servants:

He keeps us secure
He gives us strength
He leads us confidently
He sustains us in difficulty
He warns us when we stray
He forgives when we sin and confess
He is our Good Shepherd.

And we belong to God the Father, for Christ is God's Son. Guaranteeing our eternal security are:

God's sovereign authority and power
God's providential care
God's righteousness in our character
God's wisdom on life's journey
God's will and purpose for our lives.

All things belong to the Christian. Claim them, use them, enjoy them, dedicate them.

Adoniram Judson once said, "Nothing I possess has value except as it is related to the kingdom of God in Christ."

Everything we possess has value and significance as it is related to the kingdom of God.

We may hardly aspire, as William Blake,

> To see a world in a grain of sand,
> And heaven in a wild flower,
> Hold Infinity in the palm of your hand
> And eternity in an hour.

But we can agree with the great astronomer Kepler as he says: "My wish is that I may perceive the God whom I find everywhere in the external world, in like manner within and inside me."

God's Word

God created man in his own image, in the image of God created he him; male and female created he them. And God blessed them and said to them, "Be fruitful and multiply and fill the earth and subdue it; and have dominion over the fish of the sea and over the birds of the air and over every living thing that moves upon the earth."

—Genesis 1:27–28

All things are yours . . .
The world, life, death, the present or the future,
Everything is yours!
For you belong to Christ, and Christ belongs to God!

—1 Corinthians 3:21–23

Seek ye first the kingdom of God, and his righteousness; and all these things shall be added unto you.

—Matthew 6:33, KJV

A Prayer

O God, Creator, Provider, Redeemer, Father,
We claim all your blessings:
Material, personal, spiritual.
We cannot use them aright

Unless you provide your grace
And give your wisdom
And add your power
To our lives and to our actions.
May it be so. In Christ's name. Amen.

NOTES
1. Jean Holzhauer, "The Baptist Program" September, 1967.

13.
LIGHTS AND SHADOWS

Among those persons who made the greatest contributions to my own life was Harvey Eugene Dana, my New Testament professor during seminary days. I became intimately acquainted with him also prior to my student career when I served as his staff associate in a church where he was serving as interim pastor.

An essay, thought to be among the last expressions that came from the pen of H. E. Dana, was entitled "Lights and Shadows on the Canvas of Life." One of his daughters was an amateur artist. Looking at one of her unfinished pictures, he remarked to her that it was not as good as she usually painted. She answered, "That picture is not yet completed. I haven't put the shadows in it yet. No picture is complete without both lights and shadows."

He saw in this a marvelous parable of life. It takes both lights and shadows to make life's picture complete. We may think of life as a vast canvas on which an unseen hand is painting. Dana said some would call that hand fate; he insisted upon calling it Providence. "It is the very hand of God. For the portrait he is painting there to be best, the various colors must be properly blended. The picture must carry upon it both lights and shadows. Upon the canvas of every life there are both the lights and the shadows, and the shadows are just as necessary as are the brighter hues," my teacher affirmed. Dana enumerated some of the shadows that come into the lives of all of us: suffering, sorrow, disappointment, and failure. We cannot avoid them. They come irresistibly, sometimes creeping stealthily upon the canvas; sometimes splashing the dark color into the picture by one sudden unwarned stroke.

He added, "The lights also are always there." Among these are love, service, ambition, and hope. Whatever the position or station of the life, these four lights will always be casting their gentle glow, he affirmed. He emphasized especially the necessity for hope in one's life: "When its genial light dies out, life is all darkness. When hope is gone, into its place comes cynical despair, or worse yet—the ghastly spectre of the suicidial hand. But even when the future appears black, the unquenched rays of persistent hope beat their way on through the shadows and intimate some blessed vale of relief that will be revealed in glory when the fogs have lifted."

What are some of the shadows that have crossed your own life?

Maybe it was poverty. Our family—a widowed mother and six children—tilled the soil on a small farm to supply enough food and clothing for the family. Mother would go to work in the field with a hoe in the morning returning about eleven o'clock to prepare a quick lunch for the family. After washing the dishes she would go back to the field and work until time to prepare dinner. On wash day she scrubbed the clothes in the morning and then hoed corn in the afternoon. We were poor but we didn't know we were poor.

As Sam Levenson said of his childhood, spent in a slum area of Brooklyn, "Sociologists have designated people in our situation as underprivileged, but we did not know we were underprivileged." The love of parents and the spirit of hope and optimism lighted the dark shadows made by poverty. Industry and frugality and thanksgiving for what we had made life radiant.

Perhaps the shadow was oppression. Multitudes of black people in America have found it impossible to rise above their situation because they had no place to take hold. That is why they responded to Martin Luther King's voice when he said, "I have been to the mountain, and I have a dream." Because he had faith and hope he saw a brighter day ahead. The foregleams of human rights drove back many of the dark shadows of oppression and neglect.

Illness in the family may be the shadow across your path. Some dear friends of ours rejoiced at the birth of a son late in their lives. Soon they realized he was born a cystic fibrosis victim. For seven years they watched over him carefully and gave him every treatment possible in the attempt to save his life. Finally his weakened body gave in, and he breathed his last.

These were agonizing years in many ways for the parents. On the other hand, they speak tenderly of "life with little Martin." Because of their unselfish love and devotion during these years their faith was deepened, God was made more real, and heaven was brought nearer.

Imprisonment in war time has cast its ugly shadows over the lives of multitudes of people. Dachau, Auschwitz, Treblinka, and Maidanek are horrible examples of such shadows. Psychiatrist Viktor Frankl has shared some of the experiences he faced in the concentration camp at Auschwitz.

Frankl did not permit the shadows to destroy his life. Out of these experiences came his method of psychotherapy which he termed *logotherapy.* By that term he meant the spiritual aspect of life or the meaning and purpose which life holds.

He tells of facing a man and woman who were close to suicide. Both had told him that they expected nothing more of life. He asked his fellow prisoners whether the question was really what they expected of life. Was it not, rather, what life was expecting from them. This challenge to find meaning in life inspired both of them who ultimately were released from prison to go on to fulfill their life's calling.

Frankl said, "Men can give meaning to their lives by realizing what I call creative values in achieving worthwhile tasks. But they can also give meaning to their lives by realizing experiential values, by experiencing the good, the true, and the beautiful, or by knowing one single human being in all his uniqueness." He went on to say that the religious man finds life a mission and the source of that mission is God.

The supreme shadow that has crossed the life of man throughout history was the shadow of the cross of Jesus Christ. The background of the cross is the world overshadowed by the darkness of sin. The marvelous light which God blended with that darkness was the light of the resurrection of Jesus Christ.

> The whole world was lost in the darkness of sin,
> The light of the world is Jesus;
> Like sunshine at noonday His glory shown in,
> The light of the world is Jesus.

God's Word
The people who walked in darkness
Have seen a great light;
Those who dwelt in a land of deep darkness,
On them has light shined.

—Isaiah 9:2

Again Jesus spoke to them, saying, "I am the light of the world; he who follows me will not walk in darkness, but will have the light of life."

—John 8:12

In the beginning was the Word, and the Word was with God, and the Word was God. . . . In him was life and the life was the light of men. The light shines in the darkness, and the darkness has not overcome it."

—John 1:1,4–5

A Prayer
Lord, source of all light,
Give us the vision
To see the shadows clearly

Wisdom to keep them in perspective
Courage to endure them
And faith to cast light upon them,
Thus completing a masterpiece of meaning
On the canvas of life,
According to your purpose.

                                        Amen.

14.
YOU CAN'T OVERLOAD GOD

One night as I lay awake wrestling with certain problems, my mind turned to prayer. All of a sudden, I found myself saying, "There surely are a lot of these problems. I hope this is not too much to dump on God." Then I almost laughed aloud at such an absurd thought.

Soon outstanding promises from God's Word began flooding my mind: "Cast your burden on the Lord, and he will sustain you"; "Come unto me all you who labor and are heavy-laden, and I will give you rest"; "God is our refuge and strength, a very present help in trouble." When these problems took hold, my tensions began to fade, my restless muscles relaxed, and I was soon asleep.

You really can't overload God. Our heaviest burdens are nothing compared to his grace and power. He can ease the greatest burden and can even "chain" Satan so that his powers are canceled out.

Remember the story of Job? God permitted Satan to tempt, harass, and inflict pain on Job, and even to bring death to Job's children. But certain limitations were placed on Satan. God had power to restrain him.

When Martin Luther and his friend Philip Melanchthon were in prison facing execution, Luther said, "Philip, let us sing the forty-sixth Psalm." He was referring to his great hymn, "A Mighty Fortress," based on Psalm 46:

A mighty fortress is our God,
A bulwark never failing;
Our helper He, amid the flood
Of mortal ills prevailing:
For still our ancient foe
Doth seek to work us woe;
His craft and power are great,
And, armed with cruel hate,
On earth is not his equal.

God is indeed our fortress, like an impregnable fort which the enemy finds impossible to penetrate. Ancient castles were placed on inaccessible rocks and secured with gates of iron, "but God is a far better refuge from distress than all these. . . . Soldiers of the cross remember this and count yourselves safe and make yourselves strong in God." [1]

God is also our strength. Not only does he protect us, but his strength flows into us to give us power personally. Paul said, "I can do all things through Christ who continually pours his strength into me" (Phil. 4:13). The Christian actually feels the strength of Christ flowing through his own personhood.

God is our present help. He is always there in time of need. He is not an absentee God. He is readily available, as near as your prayer telephone. He never goes on strike; he is always listening. In the time of trouble he is the one all-sufficient source to which the Christian can turn.

As I read Psalm 46 many years ago certain insights were indelibly impressed upon my mind concerning God who is our help.

In the first place, we should be honest to acknowledge our need of God's help. Even the strongest man at times feels weak in the presence of his trials. It is not a sign of manhood necessarily to deny our weaknesses, to refuse to cry out to God for help. I am not ashamed to admit that at times I have found myself in tears acknowledging that I had come to the end of my rope. It is no disgrace for a strong man to weep. Jesus himself wept. He often called upon the Father for help.

In the second place, we must be sensible to recognize God's ability to help. Today it is often quite fashionable to deny the supernatural in life. Skepticism and agnosticism are first cousins to outright atheism. Even honest doubters still recognize God's ability to provide the help they need.

Furthermore, we need to be still to know the God of help. Although none can worthily proclaim his majesty, all can bow before him in adoration and praise.

Spurgeon urged his fellow Christians to be still as to words, not speaking against God's providences or complaining about them. We must also be still as to our actions and our behavior so as not to oppose God in his decrees. We must be still as to the inward attitudes of our heart, cultivating a calm and quiet submission of our souls to the will of God our Creator and Father.

The command for us to be still before God means we should relax and be calm, withdraw and quit fighting when we realize our own inabilities. It means that we are to wait with patience and trust God.

As John Bunyan said, "He who runs from God in the morning will scarcely find him through the day."

Take time to be holy, Let Him be thy guide
And run not before Him, whatever betide;
In joy or in sorrow Still follow thy Lord,
And looking to Jesus, Still trust in His Word.

God's Word

God is our refuge and strength,
A very present help in trouble.

Therefore we will not fear
Though the earth should change,
Though the mountains shake
In the heart of the sea;
Though its waters roar and foam,
Though the mountains tremble with its tumult.
Be still, and know that I am God.
I am exalted among the nations,
I am exalted in the earth!
The Lord of hosts is with us;
The God of Jacob is our refuge.

—Psalm 46:1–3,10–11

Cast your burden on the Lord
And he will sustain you;
He will never permit
The righteous to be moved.

—Psalm 55:22

Come to me, all who labor and are heavy-laden, and I will give you rest. Take my yoke upon you, and learn from me; for I am gentle and lowly of heart, and you will find rest for your souls. For my yoke is easy and my burden is light.

—Matthew 11:28–30

A Prayer

O God, Our helper,
We praise you:
For your power to create and to destroy
For your purpose to build a holy kingdom
For your love of unlimited depths
For your action in today's world.
We ask you to give us:
Direction for right living
Strength for effective service

Patience to wait for your signals
   Faith to trust you without limitation.

Amen.

NOTES

1. Charles Hadden Spurgeon, *The Treasury of David* (New York: Funk and Wagnalls, 1882), Vol. 2, p. 379.

15.
HOW IS YOUR PROFILE?

John Barrymore, the actor, was inordinately proud of his profile. His classic face had stirred the hearts of theater-goers and turned the heads of innumerable beautiful women.

The story goes that once when he was ill and had been rushed to the hospital, he asked the doctor, "Is this the final curtain?" The doctor replied, "We must all be prepared to meet our maker face-to-face." To which Barrymore replied, "I will meet him in profile."

Although this declaration was half-humorous, it is a parable on the Christian life. Many of us assume that we can face God "in profile." In other words, we want to place our best foot forward, present our finest qualities and expect God to accept us on this basis.

All the while there may be many blind spots or weaknesses or sins in our character which would not look good "in profile." What does your Christian profile show?

Pride or humility? One of the earliest memory verses I recall from my childhood declares, "Pride goes before destruction and a haughty spirit before a fall" (Prov. 16:18). Jesus reminded his disciples, "Everyone who exalts himself will be humbled, and he who humbles himself will be exalted" (Luke 14:11).

Ambition or vocation? An old adage goes, "Hitch your wagon to a star." Normal ambition is a very healthy part of man's personhood, but unbridled ambition, filled with selfish motivation, may cancel out all of the good things a man seeks to do. Life is more than ambition; it is vocation under God.

When ambition to "succeed" becomes the dominant motivation of life, God's purpose may be thwarted. Theologian Karl Barth says that calling is the "presupposition of all Christian experience." Scottish scholar James A. Robinson confirms that calling or vocation is "the supreme category of religion."

Hatred or love? A contemporary psychologist wrote a book entitled "Love Against Hate." These two attitudes are always a part of the person himself. You and I sometimes permit hostilities to build up so that our profile actually becomes hatred rather than love. Love must be cultivated and hate must be transformed. Hatred makes an ugly profile; love presents a beautiful profile to God and to man.

Cowardice or courage? Bob Gauchie was called "The man who refused to die." On February 2 just inside the Arctic Circle in Canada's Northwest Territories, Bob Gauchie set his engine down in a snowstorm. For fifty-eight days in temperatures as low as sixty below zero, and almost without food, this bush pilot fought back, determined to survive. He trudged out an SOS signal in the snow and waited. Once during that period he wrote: "Terrible cold week. Not much time for rescue now. I hope I can make peace with God. I love you girls. Pen won't write. Please pray for me."

At the end of fifty-eight days when a plane finally came to his rescue, "limping toward the turbo prop—a haggard creature with shaggy hair, one foot wrapped in dirty canvas and a bearded, emaciated face, lighted by a shining grin"—Gauchie said, "Hello, do you have room for a passenger?" Geniune Christian courage is a gift from God.

Doubt or faith? The poet Tennyson once wrote;

There lives more faith in honest doubt,
Believe me, than in half the creeds.

The poet was not encouraging doubt against faith. He simply acknowledged that doubt is a part of man's normal experience. Unless man raises questions he will never find answers. But doubt should never dominate the life. Honest doubt will lead to honest faith, and honest faith is the true Christian profile. Let us cultivate faith, even if we have to say, "Lord I believe; help my unbelief."

Despair or hope? A man came to my door and asked, "Are you the Baptist preacher?" After I invited him in, he said, "Preacher I am a terrible sinner. I seem not to be able to overcome my worst of all habits, gambling. It is about to destroy me. Is there any hope for a man like me?" I shall never forget the joy and confidence written on his face after we had talked about God's grace and had prayed for his forgiveness. He now walked with confidence in the belief that his hope was not in his own strength but in Christ who had redeemed him.

My hope is built on nothing less
Than Jesus blood and righteousness;
I dare not trust the sweetest frame
But wholly lean on Jesus name.

Selfishness or stewardship? The original painting, "The Rich Young Ruler" by Hoffmann hangs in the Riverside Church, New York. The artist captured the inner attitude of the young man which shows on his face. He is both selfish and sorrowful. He loves his riches so much he cannot give them up, and yet he is sorrowful because he rejects the lordship of Jesus Christ in his life.

Wealthy or poor one's inner attitude may be selfish concerning material values. The poor who become bitter and cynical present a profile before God almost as pathetic as that of a very rich man who places self first.

God's Word

We shall all stand before the judgment seat of God, for it is written, "As I live, says the Lord, every knee shall bow to me, every tongue shall give praise to God." So each of us shall give account of himself to God.

—Romans 14:10b–12

Let love be genuine; hate what is evil, hold fast to what is good; love one another with brotherly affection; outdo one another in showing honor. Never flag in zeal, be aglow with the Spirit, serve the Lord. Rejoice in your hope, be patient in tribulation, be constant in prayer. Contribute to the needs of the saints, practice hospitality.

—Romans 12:9–13

A Prayer

All-wise God,
You see us as we really are
We cannot hide from you
We do not present ourselves as perfect
We would like to appear before you with integrity
Give us self-understanding
That we may grow in the graces
Which will make us beautiful in your Spirit
So that we may stand in full view before you
And not in mere, sorry profile.

Amen.

16.
RELIGION AS CREATIVE INSECURITY

Recently a missionary couple were informed by their family physician that their little baby was probably a mongoloid and would never develop as a normal child.

A pastor watched beside the bed of his eleven-year-old daughter dying of leukemia. She asked him, "Daddy, will they find a cure for leukemia?" Again she asked, "Daddy, will they make me well?" They prayed for her earnestly, but she died.

A little six-year-old boy was run over during Vacation Bible School and killed. His mother and father were faithful members of the church. In their agony they wondered what they had done "to deserve" such a tragedy.

In each of these situations, God's faithful people probably asked, "Is religion security?" This is a question every one of us has asked at one time or another. This question was asked long ago by the prophet, "Is there no balm in Gilead? Is there no healing for my people?"

Peter A. Bertocci, professor of philosophy at Boston University since 1952, wrote a book entitled *Religion as Creative Insecurity*.

In a class in Philosophy of Religion I heard Professor Bertocci give his personal testimony of redemption in Christ. His faith was anchored secure in Christ.

In his book he wrote, "To flee from insecurity is to miss the whole point of being human. It is to miss the whole point of religion and of the Christian faith in particular."

Is religion security? Life has some negative answers.

It is not security in the sense that it releases us from law and moral responsibility. The Christian religion does not "emancipate man from the moral law of God." Eighteenth-century Lord Byron wrote of Childe Harold, the handsome young decadent who was

Grown aged in a world of woe
In deeds, not years, piercing the depths of life
So that no wonder awaits him.

We can't get rid of tensions by selfish indulgence.

Religion is not security as a "peace of mind" cult. So long as there are crosses to be borne, there is no place for apathy and uneasy peace of mind. Shallow sentimentalism is no substitute for genuine Christian faith.

Religion is not security as mere other-worldliness, a piety which seeks to escape from the realities of this world. Hinduism, Christian Science, Zen Buddhism, and other mystical religions are too sentimental and romanticist. The Christian faith is more than a shelter; it is a battlefield.

The Christian faith does not propose to grant full understanding concerning the will of God. Someone has said that God is the great doer of the unexpected. Indeed, "we walk by faith not by sight."

There are also some affirmative answers to the question, Is religion security? The Christian faith offers some positive answers.

S. I. Hayakawa, president, San Francisco State College, states there are two views on emotional security, namely, the static and the dynamic. The static view may be pictured by thinking of the oyster inside its shell, France before World War II behind its

Maginot Line, the frightened person behind his neurotic defenses.

The dynamic concept of security may be pictured by thinking of a skilful driver on his way home on a busy freeway. He knows there are dangers but he is not insecure. He is not frightened because he depends on inner mental resources—skill, knowledge, experience, flexibility—to help him cope with the danger.

Religion is security when it is based on faith in a God of purpose. Joshua said to his people Israel, "Our God will fight for us." Missionary Hudson Taylor once said, "All God's giants have been weak men who did great things for God because they reckoned on him as being with them."

Religion is security when it finds a challenge in life's noble endeavors, in the divine mission into which one is called. Commitment to God's purpose brings out the best that is in the Christian.

Several years ago President Nathan Pusey of Harvard University, in a baccalaureate address, said, "Religion answers the important questions by supplying meaning to life, by kindling hope, and by giving through faith in God a basis for ethical behavior."

Religion is security when it provides the believer ultimate personal victory in Christ. Paul said, "I know whom I have believed and am persuaded that he is able to keep that which I have committed to him against that day."

Religion is creative security when the Christian participates in the sufferings of Christ as achieved in the cross. Peter Bertocci declared that in the cross we are brought to the "value of values, to the pearl of great price, the creativity of forgiving love."

God's Word

I know whom I have believed and I am sure that he is able to guard until that Day what has been entrusted to me. Follow the pattern of the sound words you have heard from me, in the faith and love which are in Christ Jesus; guard the truth that has been entrusted to you by the Holy Spirit who dwells within us.

—2 Timothy 1:12–14

We have this treasure in earthen vessels, to show that the transcendent power belongs to God and not to us. . . . So we always are of good courage; . . . for we walk by faith and not by sight.

—2 Corinthians 4:7; 5:6–7.

A Prayer

O God, Source and Ground of our being,
May we not seek security
In our powers of reason
In the level of our feelings
In our human institutions
In our personal achievements
But in your redemptive love
Provided in the death and resurrection of Jesus.

Amen.

17.
INTERCESSORY PRAYER GOD'S GIFT

More things are wrought by prayer
Than this world dreams of.
Wherefore, let thy voice
Rise like a fountain for me night and day.
For what are men better than sheep or goats
That nourish a blind life within the brain,
If, knowing God, they lift not hands of prayer
Both for themselves and those who call them friend?
For so the whole round earth is every way
Bound with gold chains about the feet of God.[1]

Do you share the faith of Tennyson? Do you believe that prayer changes things? Does something really happen to other people when we pray for them? When a loved one is suffering from illness or is in danger, does prayer for that one really help? Does it make any difference whether we pray for God's kingdom to come into the life of our world?

Jesus believed in intercessory prayer. He was constantly praying for people. He told Peter, "I have prayed for you that your faith fail not." In his high-priestly prayer in the upper room he prayed for his disciples. On the cross he prayed for the multitudes, "Father, forgive them, for they know not what they do."

The man who led in my ordination service Dr. T. L. Holcomb believed in intercessory prayer. When he retired from an active job he said he decided to enter upon a new vocation, intercessory prayer. In the years that followed multitudes of people wrote to him requesting that he pray for them. He received numerous letters thanking him for his prayers and indicating that God had answered many of them.

If we are honest, we must acknowledge there are problems concerning intercessory prayer. If God knows what is best for people, why should I pray for them? Does God's blessings on other persons depend upon my prayers? How can God use my prayers to affect the other person? How can we know that intercessory prayers are really answered?

On the positive side, God has commanded us to pray for one another. Augustine said, "Without God, we cannot; without us, God will not." Concerning some things God depends upon our prayers.

Archbishop Temple said that he could raise more problems about intercessory prayer than he could ever answer. He went on to say, "When I pray for my brother wondrous things happen." These may be coincidences, he acknowledged. However, when he prays for his brother, these coincidences occur, and when he does not pray for him, these coincidences do not occur.

In intercessory prayer there is shared community. The Model Prayer Jesus taught his disciples to pray is the quintessence of prayer, and it is prayer in community. It begins, "*Our* Father" and not "*My* Father."

Persons in the fellowship of Christ are linked together through prayer. Prayer is communion with God, and when two persons are in communion with God, even though they may be in different places, there is a conscious fellowship of love.

He who prays for another doubtless becomes a better man. His own faith is strengthened and his love deepened.

One of the best ways to be forgiving is to pray for the person who has offended you.

Bonhoeffer wrote there is no way from one person to another. We cannot penetrate the incognito of the other man, for there are no direct relationships between soul and soul. But Christ stands in between to create a unity of persons.[2]

Prayer influences the other person. God has created us to be a community of persons. Doubtless, God makes the other person conscious that we are praying for him.

In intercessory prayer we take on the yoke of Christ as we share his life work and pray in union with him. George Stewart said, "If our intercessions are to be a real sharing of the work of Christ they demand earnestness of will and openness to his spirit and love for others." [3]

God's Word

[Christ] is able for all time to save those who draw near to God through him, since he always lives to make intercession for them.

—Hebrews 7:25

Pray at all times in the Spirit, with all prayer and supplication. To that end keep alert with all perseverance, making supplication for all the saints, and also for me. . . . That I may declare [the gospel] boldly as I ought to speak.

—Ephesians 6:18–20

A Prayer

Our Father, teach us to pray
For the lost and straying
That they may be forgiven;
For our neighbors in need
That they may have life's necessities;
For enemies that would do us harm
That they may learn of your grace and mercy;
For your witnesses and servants

That they may have power to persuade,
So that your kingdom may come
In the lives of multitudes.
In Christ's Name. Amen.

NOTES

1. Alfred Tennyson, *Idylls of the King,* "The Passing of Arthur."

2. Dietrich Bonhoeffer, *The Cost of Discipleship* (New York: Macmillan Co., 1937), p. 87.

3. George Stewart, *The Lower Levels of Prayer* (Nashville: Abingdon Press, 1939), p. 72.

18.
AN AFFAIR WITH THE FUTURE

The writer Alexander Wolcott believed in the ongoingness of life. He said facetiously he has chosen the title for his next book, *I'm in Love with the Past, But I'm Having an Affair with the Future.*

Jack Benny says he would not really like to go back to age thirty-nine even if he could. He's enjoying life too much as it is. He said that life has been good to me, and it still is.

Life really is a quest. In the history of great literature man has been challenged to reach for the noblest goals in life. John Bunyan's *Pilgrim's Progress* portrayed life as a journey. Man is only a pilgrim here.

The movie "Man from La Mancha" is based upon Cervantes' great novel *Don Quixote.* A young man bent on righting the wrongs of society is willing to "fight the impossible foe, to right the unrightable wrong, to dream the impossible dream." Nothing less can satisfy him in the quest for life.

Robert Browning wrote:

That low man seeks a little thing to do
  Sees it and does it:

This high man with a great thing to pursue
  Dies ere he knows it.

Browning went on to say that it is better to aim at a million and miss it by one than to aim at a hundred and get it.

All the ultimate goals of life are established by God himself. It is his will that man settle for nothing less than the highest and best. Life based upon the will of God is life with meaning. When man ignores the will of God, life becomes empty and purposeless.

Some people want to be rid of life. The mystic in Zen Buddhism believes that life is absorption in the All of the universe. His goal is to be rid of the responsibility of living by being taken up into Creation itself.

The Hindu mystic looks forward to Nirvanna or nothingness. In his fatalism life really becomes insignificant.

The existentialist Camus holds to the absurdity of life itself. There is no purpose, no goal, no real meaning in life. All of man's strivings are really absurd.

All such false views of life lead to discouragement, disillusionment, fatalism, and meaninglessness. The Christian has an affair with the future. Because he believes in a God of purpose, his life, created in the image of God, takes on genuine meaning. To him life is really a quest, a search for the deeper meanings, a striving for the ultimates of life.

In the Christian community life has meaning at every level. For the little child it means dependence and security in the strength of its parents. In the atmosphere of love his life is full of wonder and trust.

The growing youth finds life filled with ambition and adventure into independence. He feels he is really somebody, and he wants to become his true self. In his idealism he sees his parents as examples furnished him by God.

The young adult is in the process of establishing worthwhile goals. He is building up his confidence and seeking self-fulfillment.

He is searching for answers to life's ultimate questions.

Reuel Howe characterizes middle life as the "creative years." He believes that adults have the power within to cope with the problems and crises of life. By heeding God's command to understand, to love, and to care for others, the adult years will become the creative and most rewarding years.

Howe sees in God's redemptive action the creation of new men. Faith in God's purposes provides foundations for marriage, family, friendship, and all other great human values. The climax of this faith is a "ministering faith," one that empowers us to give ourselves in service and love to others.[1]

In the older years especially, the Christian has an affair with the future. God's elderly children reach the climax of life in which the riches of faith are more thoroughly understood and more fully enjoyed.

Life will always be an adventure for him who is ready to meet it halfway. God continues to pour out his blessings upon man so long as man is willing to open his life to receive them.

Someone has said, "God likes life; He invented it!" Throughout the Bible life is connected with God. God creates and sustains life. Without God life is nothingness; at God's command everything takes on movement and meaning.

The Christian psychiatrist Tournier said that life does not follow a straight line. Man must continue to be sensitive to the voice of God if he would continually find life an adventure. "This knowledge of God, this perpetual rediscovery of God, with its new understanding of his will, even at the cost of our faults, is the meaning of life according to the Bible," says Tournier.[2]

God's Word
See, I have set before you this day life and good, death and evil. . . .
Therefore, choose life, that you may live, you and your seed.
—Deut. 30:15,19.

I am the way, and the truth, and the life; no one comes to the Father but by me.

—John 14:6

I came that they might have life, and have it abundantly. I am the good shepherd. The good shepherd lays down his life for the sheep.

—John 10:10-11

A Prayer

Lord of life,
Show us new horizons
That we may find joy in traveling
On life's journey
Shake us loose from the dead past
So that we may be aware of the living present
And give us visions of the certain future
You have already purposed
For all who truly live in Jesus Christ.

Amen.

NOTES

1. Reuel Howe, *The Creative Years* (Greenwich, Connecticut: Seabury Press, 1959), p. 224.

2. Paul Tournier, *A Doctor's Casebook in the Light of the Bible* (New York: Harper and Bros., 1960), p. 144.

19.
I LOVE YOU

A mature business man who tries to live his Christianity visited his aged uncle who was dying of emphysema. As he prepared to leave the room, he took his uncle's hand and said, as he bent low, "I love you, Uncle Dennis." Then slowly he said, "You know I love you, don't you?" Then he repeated even more slowly, "I really do love you."

After he left, the old man turned to his sister, tears streaming down his face, and said, "He really does love me. I know he does, for he told me three times that he loves me."

"Mother, I kissed her!" the little girl said in a pleased and excited voice. The child had made a discovery that too few adults ever make. Upon impulse she had bent down and planted a kiss upon the face of an elderly resident of a rest home. She discovered that the little lady who had received her gesture of friendship was like other people—just a little older than most perhaps, and unable to live independently.[1]

The three little words "I love you" are among the most powerful ever spoken by human lips. Mothers croon them to their tiny babies. Lovers whisper them in each other's ears. Husbands and wives repeatedly remind one another of that fact. Little children enjoy telling their parents of their affection.

These words are not repeated often enough. Sometimes we allow selfishness to keep us from speaking such tenderness. Our pride stands in the way. We are afraid it will indicate weakness on our part. Or, perhaps, we may be afraid we shall lose an argument which has caused us to break fellowship with a member of the family or a friend.

Prejudices may prevent our speaking of love to persons who do not fit into our own categories. They never hear us talk of love. If they happen to be on different levels of the social register we may find it difficult to share our real feelings with them.

No one needs to hear about love more than one's enemy. Even though he may have treated you with hatred and scorn he really needs love. Genuine love is possible only when there is a true spirit of forgiveness.

Love must be cultivated. It takes a great deal of will power to express love in the face of handicaps. Love must come out of the depths of one's very character in spite of the things that hinder.

The true follower of Christ is lovable. He is not afraid to love others, and he is not ashamed to say, "I love you."

Members of the family should cultivate tenderness and affection. They should learn to reach out to one another, literally to touch one another physically as an expression of honest love.

Because parents are more mature than their children, they should take the initiative in expressing love.

Teen-agers, in their desire to become independent and to resist the authority of their parents, should determine to let love prevail. Cooperation and obedience are evidence of true love.

Soren Kierkegaard wrote:

What is it that makes a man immovable,
More immovable than a rock;
What is it that makes him soft,

Softer than wax?
It is love!
What is it that cannot be taken
But itself takes everything?
It is love.
What is it that cannot be given,
But itself gives everything?
It is love.
What is it that endures when all else disappoints?
It is love.
What is it that comforts when all comfort fails?
It is love.
What is it that turns the words of a simple man into wisdom?
It is love.
What is it that never changes when all else changes?
It is love.
Only that is love
Which never becomes anything else." [2]

God's Word

You have heard that it was said, "You shall love your neighbors and hate your enemies, but I say to you, love your enemy and pray for those who persecute you, so that you may be sons of your Father who is in heaven.

—Matthew 5:43–45

As the Father has loved me, so have I loved you; abide in my love. This is my commandment, that you love one another as I have loved you.

—John 15:9,12

Love one another with brotherly affection; outdo one another in showing honor.

—Romans 12:10

Faith, hope, love abide, these three; but the greatest of these is love.
—1 Corinthians 13:13

A Prayer

Our loving Father,
We thank you for your love
We offer our love to you
Cleanse us of all hate
So that love may grow
Give us the courage to love
Words to express our love
And deeds to fulfill that love
As we know its reality
In Jesus Christ our Lord. Amen.

NOTES

1. "The Second Page," Second Baptist Church, Lubbock, Texas. July 16, 1971.

2. Soren Kierkegaard. *Edifying Discourses.* Edited by Paul L. Holmer. (New York: Harper and Bros., 1958), p. 51.

20.
LEAVE IT TO THE SPIRIT

I borrowed the title of this essay from an intriguing book by John Killinger, *Leave It to the Spirit*. The author observed that many faithful church members find themselves bored with the worship services. They say, "There must be something wrong with me." They attend as a form of penance but find it like some bitter medicine which must be good for them.

Killinger appeals for a fresh approach to worship, an effort to overcome the lethargic practice in many of our churches. He urges the churches to relate their worship to the life and style of a contemporary world, becoming the MC, the poet, the toastmaster, for celebrating the presence of God and all of life.[1]

Should not you and I "leave it to the Spirit" in every area of life? The vital Christian will be alive to the Spirit, not only in the formal worship service provided by his church, but also in his own private style of life. Every sincere Christian desires to be alive to God and alert to his voice.

Jesus said the Spirit of God is the presence of God directing by his purpose and will: "The wind blows where it pleases and you hear the sound of it but you do not know where it comes from or where it goes. That is just the way it is with everyone who is born of the Spirit" (John 3:8, Williams).

God manifested, showed forth, demonstrated his living presence in the resurrection and in such outpouring of the Spirit as the action at Pentecost. The Holy Spirit is nothing more nor less than the presence of the living God in the life of the believer.

The Spirit makes the incarnational presence of God in us a reality. His presence is the presence of the living Christ in the life of the Christian. As Charles Gore once said, "The Holy Spirit comes not so much to supply the absence of Christ as to accomplish his presence."

Do you desire to be "filled with the Spirit"? Are you afraid of the power of God's Spirit? Are you ever ashamed to acknowledge that you feel the presence of the living God within you?

These are some of the things that prevent Christians from being dynamic and zealous for Christ. Because some people have perverted the doctrine of God's Spirit many Christians are afraid to acknowledge the reality of his presence.

The Holy Spirit in the Christian life does not mean a fanatical zeal concerning a certain doctrine of the Spirit. A dogmatic doctrine can lead to division and hatred. When John Calvin had Servetus burned at the stake, he said it was "for the glory of God."

An example of doctrinal and institutional fanaticism is seen in Ireland today in the Protestant-Catholic war. Hatred, and not love, prevails. As one visitor to Ireland said, "Religion is all over the place." But this is not religion according to the presence of God.

New Testament Christians laid no claim to a "pecular visitation" of the Spirit, such as some extremists have claimed. It is not a "second blessing" or any other unusual visitation. It is the most normal thing in the world for a Christian to be filled with God's Spirit.

Some churches today are disturbed over the question of *glossolalia* or "speaking in tongues." Certain people insist that one is not really filled with God's presence unless he speaks in tongues. This really is an exaggeration of individual experience which may lead to spiritual pride.

Excitement or ecstasy is not necessarily a measure of how spiritual a person is. As our professor W. T. Conner used to say, "The sign of genuine religion is not how high you jump, but how straight you walk when you hit the ground. This is the thing that counts."

The New Testament doctrine of the Holy Spirit means the breath of God, the life of God, the energizing presence of God, the inspiring power of God in the believer. The Christian is conscious of a power greater than himself.

God's presence in our lives will be evident in our worship. Raymond Abba says:

> It is through worship that the church is united by the Holy Spirit to Christ . . . and hence becomes the instrument of his saving activity in the world. . . . What matters . . . is not whether worship makes us feel good or happy; what matters is whether it makes us Christ-like; whether men take knowledge of us that we have been with Jesus.[2]

In a genuine worship experience you not only feel something, you also think something, decide something, and act upon the experience. Oh, for a fresh worship experience that will lift us above the humdrum of day-by-day activity!

The prayer life ought to be filled with the presence of God. Paul assured us that "the Spirit helps us in our weakness; for we do not know how to pray as we ought, but the Spirit himself intercedes for us with sighs too deep for words" (Rom. 8:26).

Theologian P. T. Forsyth declared that the Holy Spirit is the "grandmaster of God's art and mystery in communing with man. And there is no other teacher, at last, of man's art of communing with God."

The test of a holy life is the test of Christ-like character. The Holy Spirit bestows the virtues of Christ upon us and works with us in developing those virtues. L. M. Starky said that the Holy

Spirit is Christ's presence within us to work his life out. The virtues of Christ are the Spirit's harvest within us: love, joy, peace, patience, kindness, goodness, fidelity, gentleness, and self-control, as set forth in Galatians 5:22.

If we are to "leave it to the Spirit," we must let go of our selfish concerns and let God direct us by his wisdom. The Christian is freed to live in the freedom of the Spirit's leadership—in courage, in confidence, with poise, with a sort of zealous abandon. Not in some strange or peculiar way, not in an irrelevant manner, but with clear-eyed, reasoned, decisive action.

The test of God's Spirit within us is love. Paul said, "God's love has flooded our inmost heart through the Holy Spirit he has given us" (Rom. 5:5, NEB). God's love molds his people into a unity, a fellowship of *koinonia*.

God's Word

Now the Lord is the Spirit and where the Spirit of the Lord is, there is freedom.

—2 Corinthians 3:17

The Spirit of the Lord is upon me,
Because he has anointed me
To preach good news to the poor.
He has sent me to proclaim release to the captives
And recovering of sight to the blind,
To set at liberty those who are oppressed,
To proclaim the acceptable year of the Lord.

—Luke 4:18–19

If the Spirit is the source of our life, let the Spirit also direct our course. We must not be conceited, challenging one another to rivalry, jealous of one another.

—Galatians 5:25–26, NEB

A Prayer

Breathe on me, Breath of God,
Fill me with life anew,

That I may love what thou dost love,
And do what thou wouldst do.

Breathe on me, breath of God,
Till I am wholly Thine,
Till all this earthly part of me
Glows with thy fire divine.

Amen.

NOTES

1. John Killinger, *Leave It to the Spirit* (New York: Harper and Row, 1971), p. xvii.

2. Raymond Abba, *Principles of Christian Worship* (London: Oxford University Press, 1957), p. 13.

21.
YOU ARE NOT REALLY ALONE

Dag Hammarskjold, one-time Secretary General of the United Nations, will always be remembered as a great international civil servant. He left a sort of autobiography entitled *Markings*. In spite of his achievements there is a deep underlying sense of loneliness throughout this intimate profile of himself.[1]

He wrote:

What makes loneliness an anguish
Is not that I have no one to share my burden,
But this: I have only my own burden to bear.

Pray that your loneliness may spur you
Into finding something to live for,
Great enough to die for.

Loneliness is not a sickness unto death.
No, but can it be cured except by death?
And does it not become the harder to bear
The closer one comes to death?

For man shall commune with all creatures to his profit,
But enjoy God alone.
That is why no human being can be

A permanent source of happiness to another.

In some way we all are lonely persons. Loneliness is actually a feeling of need of other persons. There is a sort of vacuum that cannot be filled except by another human being. Perhaps God made us that way so that we would open our lives to others.

There is a sense in which a man feels himself a sensitive outsider in the universe; he realizes that "home is somewhere I have never been." Man is continually on the search for that relationship which he can call home.

Paul Tournier found himself deeply moved by "the emotional isolation of modern man." [2] In Europe and in America he found people lonely. Even though Americans love to be in groups they still have a basic loneliness. Togetherness and light-heartedness are not enough to fill that emptiness, according to Tournier.

Human life begins with a cry of lonelinesss. At the moment of birth the child is separated from the mother, and human life begins its journey of loneliness. Not only is the child lonely but in a sense the mother is also lonely, now that she is no longer carrying the babe in her body.

Everyone must begin life as an individual. He has needs which other persons can fill. In his feeling of loneliness he begins to reach out to others, trying to establish a relationship. Loneliness can sometimes become a problem, but God intended it to be a challenge.

People in places of leadership are bound to be confronted with the feeling of loneliness. I found that as a pastor I had to struggle against loneliness. There are times when only you and God can work through a problem.

I confess I have had to strive to overcome timidity and loneliness. My father died when I was ten years old. As a child I felt a loneliness that only a father could fill. As a youth I was somewhat shy because I felt that other young men had an advantage over me. They had strong fathers backing them up. Gradually and painfully through the years I learned to acknowledge my worth, to accept my own strengths, and to share them with other lonely persons.

In her book, *Conflicts of the Clergy* Margaretta Bowers, M.D., writes, "The clergy are lonely, set-apart people. Even the healthy, fulfilled, successful ones remember the loneliness of their childhood." Dr. Bowers goes on to say that too often ministers try to carry their burdens and inner turmoil alone. They do not acknowledge their own human limitations. Some of them break down because they fail to share their feelings with others.

Is it true then that everybody experiences loneliness at times? Mothers, business men, housemaids, farmers, teachers, doctors, children, young people, older people—none is exempt.

There are many causes for loneliness. Self-centeredness may produce feelings of isolation, thinking of oneself as cut off from others.

Wrong thoughts and actions towards other people have produced guilt and estrangement. Separation is the essence of guilt. To be estranged from God is the deepest of loneliness.

The inability to love, to reach out and touch another can produce deep emptiness.

Perhaps bereavement is the greatest cause of loneliness. Death brings a loss that seems almost impossible to accept.

The uniqueness of a task may demand a sort of detachedness. A prominent political leader was constantly in the midst of crowds in public life. He gained notoriety. But he felt deserted. He spent very little time with his family, and they were lonely. When he retired from public life, he said he was glad to settle down at home once more. But the children had grown up and gone, and he could not recall the scenes which he had missed during the intervening years.

Mobility brings about uprootedness for families, creating a continuous feeling of isolation. I recall our family moving when I was nine years of age. We had lived in a particular community for five years. I had started to school there. Warm friendships had developed. As we loaded the wagon and prepared to drive off, several neighbors gathered to say good-bye. Mother and the other women cried, and we children cried. Parting from friends meant separation and bereavement.

But life was not made for loneliness. It was made for adventure and fellowship. Abraham was called to leave the land of his fathers, to go forth on a journey that would lead to the fulfillment of God's will. But he was not alone. God was with him.

To know God is to know the fellowship of love. Man should learn to spend some time alone with God.

Pascal said, "All the evils of life have come upon us because men refused to sit alone quietly in a room."

God through his grace creates the power for fellowship in the hearts of people. The first step towards overcoming loneliness is a step of faith in Christ as Savior. The sin that isolates is blotted out, and one is freed for fellowship.

Perhaps the best way to overcome loneliness is to lose oneself in God's call to service. No one can long remain lonely who gives himself to others.

God's Word

I am not alone, for the Father is with me. I have said this to you, that in me you may have peace. In the world you have tribulation; but be of good cheer, I have overcome the world.

—John 16:32–33

I am not going to leave you alone in the world—I am coming to you.
—John 14:18, Phillips

It is the Lord who goes before you; he will be with you, he will not fail you or forsake you; do not fear or be dismayed.

—Deuteronomy 31:8

A Prayer

God of the lonely,
You knew loneliness

And so you created man;
In the face of the cross
You enacted resurrection;
In the shadow of death
You break forth as light!
Fill our lives with your presence
That we may find strength
To give ourselves to others
In love and fellowship.

Amen.

NOTES

1. Dag Hammarskjold's, *Markings,* Translated from Swedish by Leif Sjoberg and W. H. Auden (New York: Alfred A. Knopf, 1964), p. 85 ff.

2. Paul Tournier, *Escape from Loneliness* (Philadelphia: Westminster Press, 1962), p. 10.

22.
BREAKING DOWN BARRIERS

In his book *The Luminous Darkness,* a black minister Howard Thurman gives a personal interpretation of "the anatomy of segregation and the ground of hope." [1] Thurman writes, "When I was a boy growing up in Florida, it never occurred to me, nor was I taught either at home or in church to include white people in my world." They were not hated; they were simply tolerated. The tragedy was that there was no ethical sense of relationship between black and white people.

But prejudice did not defeat Howard Thurman. He became one of America's great preachers and writers and served for several years as Dean of the Chapel at Boston University. He also taught a course in the spiritual disciplines in the school of theology there. He declares that the hope for overcoming prejudice lies in seeing oneself a human being who loves all other human beings in Christ, regardless of color.

Thurman's wife pays a high tribute to him: "He leads men home." An example is worth a thousand arguments.

My own childhood experience sowed the seeds of prejudice. A few miles away from my farm home was a small town inhabited by black people only. They had a mill in their little village where we regularly took our corn to be ground when we ran out of meal. Sometimes we bought other staple commodities there or took a bale of cotton to the gin.

Generally speaking, however, adults conveyed the idea that *they* were different from us. Some of the people referred to the village as "nigger town." But mother would always try to correct such prejudice by teaching us to call them Negroes. And so I never had any hard prejudice. Mine was a sort of subtle prejudice mixed with the feeling of pity. I felt that we should count them friends and neighbors.

In 1797 the daughter of a country preacher, Jane Austen described middle-class life, portraying everyday characters in her novel. She gave her story the title *Pride and Prejudice,* for the two go together. Like so many other attitudes, prejudice takes its roots in pride.

Prejudice has many faces. The most obvious expression of prejudice in the world today is racial. From the headlines one gets the idea that the world is divided into racial camps warring against one another—white against black, brown against white, yellow against other colors.

Society is often divided into economic classes. Those with greater wealth are called the upper class, people a little less affluent are middle class, and the lower income groups, the lower class. As he was growing up, Woody Guthrie lived on the "other side of the tracks" from my wife's people. He felt lonely even then, somewhat isolated from the middle and upper classes economically. The high school students looked upon him and other poor persons as not belonging.

Most of us are grouped according to our mores and our morality rules. In 1965 Arab Seminary students in the Middle East believed it wrong for women to wear cosmetics or jewelry. The women missionaries often felt uncomfortable because they were accustomed to using cosmetics and adorning themselves with jewelry.

I told a class of married students that if they were to come to one of our churches in America without "makeup" on, they would be conspicious. Wearing it or not wearing it does not determine how religious one is.

Society often divides itself into higher education and lower education groups. In the early history of Southern Baptists there was a strong sentiment against educated preachers. There are still some Baptists who feel that "higher education" ruins the spirit of a preacher.

We have "high church" and "low church" Baptist churches, as indicated by their forms of worship, especially as they are expressed in cultural and esthetic values. People often choose churches and denominations on the basis of cultural and educational levels.

Narrow nationalism shows itself everywhere in the world. Not all of us in America exemplify the spirit of the welcome written on the base of the Statue of Liberty. Other countries also have their problems. Our son Sam, his wife Linda, and their little daughter Breanna are living in Switzerland where he is engaged in an international research project in high energy physics. The language barrier stands between them and their neighbors. Many of the people there seem to resent Americans who do not know their language.

Sometimes there is prejudice between professions. Often as I discuss the value of medical treatment of emotional problems, some seminary students react with prejudice against psychiatrists. Reacting against Freud's agnosticism, they assume that all psychiatrists are anti-Christian. Gradually ministers and doctors are learning to work together as a healing team.

Narrow political partisanship is one of the ugliest examples of prejudice in America today. A Democrat is against a Republican president, and a Republican is against a Democratic president, regardless of the character of the president himself. The partisanship of political leaders often reflects an irrational prejudice that creates a credibility gap between them and the general public.

Perhaps the worst of all prejudice is religious prejudice. Most of us are horrified today over the bigotry in the war between Catholics and Protestants in Ireland. But we have a great deal of religious prejudice here in America. In the community where I grew up the Methodists tolerated the Baptists, and the Baptists tolerated the Methodists and the so-called "Campbellites." And all of them knew that a Catholic could not possibly get to heaven.

W. A. Sangster quotes a Roman Catholic as pronouncing "sure damnation for everyone outside the Roman Church." [2] Sangster asks, "Did Father Murphy know nothing of the saints of other communions? Had he never heard of Richard Baxter and George Herbert; or Josephine Butler and Catharine Booth; or John Keble and Frank Crossley; or Charles Hadden Spurgeon or Alexander White? These lived lives that were lovely and they did it in the name of Jesus Christ."

One may also ask whether bigoted Protestants never heard anything of the great Christians of the Roman Church: Saint Francis of Assisi, Brother Lawrence, Father Damien, priest among the lepers, Baron von Hugel, writer of devotional classics, Bernard of Clairvaux, author of "Jesus, the Very Thought of Thee" and "Jesus, Thou Joy of Loving Hearts."

Sangster calls attention to the fact that in the worst ages of bigotry, there were "lovely deeds of magnanimous affection which shine like jewels in the dark story of the past." When Richard Baxter, Puritan pastor at Kidderminster was condemned at the age of seventy by the notorious Judge Jeffreys, after an unjust trial, he was befriended by a Roman Catholic peer. Baxter was thrown into prison because he could not pay an impossible fine of five hundred marks, but was finally set at liberty through the efforts of Lord Powis.

Baxter himself was a great lover of freedom. Later the citizens from the various churches in Kidderminster contributed towards a fund and erected a monument to Baxter which stands today at a cross section in the village of Kidderminster.

Prejudice can be overcome. Since prejudice means prejudging, it is necessary to gather all the facts and face the whole truth in any situation where prejudice is at work.

Our prejudice must also be seen in the light of the gospel and the Christian ethic. There is no room in the Christian gospel for racial discrimination or any other prejudice against our fellowman.

It is the duty of every Christian to develop the habit of thinking of others as he believes God thinks of them. If we think God's thought after him, we shall increase our respect and love for every person.

Only the grace of God can finally eradicate the sin of prejudice. The Holy Spirit can cause bigotry to melt away and warm the heart and deepen the compassion, so that all men see one another as brothers in Christ.

William Barkley said, "The plain truth emerges that if a man does not find God in his fellow men, he does not find God at all."

I sought my soul, my soul I could not see;
I sought my God, my God eluded me;
I sought my brother, and I found all three.[3]

God's Word

For he is himself our peace. Gentiles and Jews, he has made the two one, and in his own body of flesh and blood has broken down the enmity which stood like a dividing wall between them.

—Ephesians 2:14–15, NEB

God is no respecter of persons.

—Acts 10:34, KJV

Judge not, that you be not judged.

—Matthew 7:1

A Prayer

God of every man,
Make us willing

To face the facts of our humanity,
To recognize all men as brothers
For whom Christ died,
To right the wrongs of prejudice,
And to cultivate a feeling of unity
In the Spirit of Jesus Christ our Lord.

Amen.

NOTES

1. Howard Thurman, *The Luminous Darkness* (New York: Harper and Row, 1965), p. 3.

2. W. A. Sangster, *He Is Able* (London: Wyvern Books, 1958), p. 118.

3. William Barkley, *In the Hands of God* (New York: Harper and Row, 1966), p. 46.

23.
ECOLOGICAL HOPE

Space scientist Edward B. Lindaman forecasts new directions for man in space:

Permanent orbiting hospitals

Health resorts a few hundred miles above earth

Cosmodromes as way stations

Tourist flights to the moon

Skyscrapers five times higher than the Empire State

Suspension bridges twice as long as today's longest

Space science and air and water pollution

Conversion of wastes and litter through space science

Earthquake prediction through information from space

Weather forecasting dominated by data from space

Increased and higher quality food production

Better use of natural resources to avert world famine.[1]

Lindaman goes on to say that knowledge gained from space will prove to be that "midcourse correction" in man's relationship with the environment and with his fellowman.

These predictions sound fantastic to the average layman. Only a space scientist can dream like this and have confidence that his dreams will come true.

Perhaps you and I also may develop ecological hope. Ecology is defined as the science of relationships between organisms and their environments. Our primary concern here is with man and his environment. Or, as someone has said, man's relationship to the various support systems of the world on which he depends for his life. Specifically this involves the air, the earth, and the water.

A specialist in the field of nursery science says that plants, trees and shrubs not only bring beauty to the world of man—they may save his life. He declares that man can live for weeks without food, for days without water, but only for minutes without oxygen. Plants produce oxygen which man and the animal kingdom breathe to stay alive, and the animal kingdom throws off carbon dioxide which plants convert to food and release in the form of oxygen.

When astronauts Borman, Anders, and Lovell during Apollo 8 space flight around the moon decided to read a passage from the Bible, they chose the opening passage of the book of Genesis: "God created the heavens and the earth." Bill Anders wrote later, "When we thought about the vastness of the world, we decided to read a message that did not belong to any one religion but which belonged to all men on earth, the story of our creation."

The psalmist wrote, "The earth is the Lord's and the fullness thereof, the world and those who dwell therein" (Psalms 24:1). Man is a part of those who dwell upon the earth. Man is a creature, involved in creatureliness, just as the physical cosmos and the animals are creaturely. He is a part of his environment.

A contemporary poet Rod McKuen loves nature and the animal kingdom—dogs, cats, turtles, and raccoons. He said, "Whether one is planting love or lima beans, he must follow his furrow carefully."

Man views the earth and all of its majestic splendor just as it was fashioned by the Creator. The earth really is man's to enjoy and to use.

But there is also a dark side to man and his ecological environment. When man exploits the earth by wiping out vast areas of plant life, by dumping great volumes of waste materials into rivers and oceans, or by turning loose poisonous gases into the atmosphere, the resulting pollution becomes man's enemy which he himself has created.

When Gemini pilot Pete Conrad shot pictures of the earth he said, "Notice the air pollution drifting out there nearby in case anybody thinks we don't have it."

Lindaman reminds us of our "troubled waters." [2] He said that the rivers have exactly the same amount of water as they did before man's time: no more, no less. The problem is that no longer do many of them provide usable water. He remarks that many big power companies and manufacturing plants act as if they consider themselves divine in the use of natural resources.

A new respect for nature is essential for man in the space age. We must realize once again that the good earth is a gift from God. The proper use of it is our solemn stewardship.

Perhaps Dr. Albert Schweitzer went too far in his reverence for all living things, but at least he reminds us of the need to have greater consideration for nature. Francis of Assisi may have been a romanticist when he spoke of "brother sun, mother earth and sister moon," but he calls all of us back to our kinship with our earth home.

We need to develop new patterns of neighborliness in an overcrowded world where one man's "food" may be another man's "poison." As Lindaman says, today the atmosphere is everybody's business, and the careless philosophy of "pollute thy neighbor" must stop.

Above all, God's people must have a renewal of faith in the God of creation and thus develop ecological hope. If we use God's gifts properly and ask for his guidance, a yet more meaningful use of the world's vast resources will result.

If we have lost the capacity for holy thoughts we still "possess a rage for reciprocity, for a universe of presence, for intimations of the holiness of rocks, trees, machines, and ourselves." [3] Heyen pleads for a theological understanding of our world.

Like the poet Roethke every man may come to "conceive the world in sacramental terms, as radiant presence, hail it and be hailed by it, hear the inner songs of snails, continent and self coming always nearer to a Being at ease with itself." [4] The Christian understands this Being is God, and to be in harmony with God is to be at home in the universe.

René Dubois wrote in *The American Scholar:* "One of the hopeful aspects of our time is the widespread acknowledgment that, if things are in the saddle, it is because we put them there. The situation, however, is not irreversible." We can do something about it.

God's Word

When I look at thy heavens, the work of thy fingers,
The moon and the stars which thou hast established;
What is man that thou art mindful of him,
And the son of man that thou dost care for him?
Yet thou hast made him little less than God,
And dost crown him with glory and honor.
Thou hast given him dominion over the works of thy hands;
Thou hast put all things under his feet,
All sheep and oxen
And also the beasts of the field,
The birds of the air,
The fish of the sea,
Whatever passes along the paths of the sea.
O, Lord, our Lord,
How majestic is thy name in all the earth!

—Psalm 8:3–9

The creation waits with eager longing for the revealing of the sons of God; for the creation was subjected to futility, not of its own will but by the will of him who subjected it in hope; because the creation itself will be set free from its bondage to decay and obtain the glorious liberty of the children of God. We know that the whole creation has been groaning in travail together until now.

—Romans 8:19–22

Consider the lilies of the field, how they grow;
They neither toil nor spin;
Yet I tell you, even Solomon in all his glory
Was not arrayed like one of these.

—Matthew 6:28*b*–19

A Prayer

O Lord, Creator of heaven and earth,
You made us in your image
You made us a part of all your creation
You gave us the beautiful, rich world for our use
You put us in charge of all the earth.
Forgive our careless use of our world
Give us wisdom to set things right
Give us love to share the world with our neighbors
Give us hope for a better world to come.

Amen.

NOTES

1. Edward B. Lindaman, *Space: A New Direction for Mankind* (New York: Harper and Row, 1969).

2. *Op. cit.,* p. 70.

3. William Heyen, *Saturday Review,* May 22, 1971, p. 33.

4. *Ibid.,* p. 49.

24.
WHERE THE ACTION IS

"I want to be where the action is" is heard on every hand. The human race seems to be divided into action groups or action fronts.

This may refer to the war front, the political front, the youth front, the racial front, the ecological front, the religious front. It refers to changes and sometimes revolution.

The Christian is faced with a primary question. Does "where the action is" refer to the action of man or the action of God? The important question for the people of God is "Where is God at work?" That's where the church wants to be and where the individual Christian feels called to be.

On July 31, 1971 when Jim Irwin and Dave Scott were in their moon buggy on their way to Hadley's Crater, they were not certain of their location. Commentator John Chancellor said, "They know where they are going, but they don't know where they're at." But they kept on going and finally located Elbow Crater. There they got their bearings and went on with their mission.

Perhaps we modern Christians, confronted with such a vast amount of work to be done, don't know where we're at, but by faith we keep our spiritual radar sensitive to God's direction, where the action is.

Recently in a magazine article the question was asked, "If you learned that Jesus Christ was in your city in the flesh as he was two thousand years ago, where would you expect to find him—in the church, or out in the world serving humanity?

The article went on to imply that he would not be in the church, the "establishment," but out in the world serving the needs of humanity.

The New Testament story of Jesus's ministry gives us some clues as to where the action is where Jesus himself is concerned. He will be found today exactly where he was found during his ministry in the flesh. The gospel story gives a clear picture of where the action is according to Jesus. That's where you and I would like to be in today's world.

According to the New Testament Jesus was found in the church at worship. His family took him to worship in his early childhood. In those days the people of God could be heard singing a song of ascent on their way up to the Temple: "I will look unto the hills, from whence cometh my help. My help cometh from the Lord who made heaven and earth!" Jesus must have joined in the hymn of praise.

Jesus went to the synagogue on the sabbath day, as the custom was, and there read the Word of God, joined in prayers, and sang hymns with his people.

Jesus is found in dialogue with students, with learners. At twelve years of age he went to the Temple to discuss important issues with the teachers. He often challenged the lawyers and scribes of his day by asking, "What do you think?" He was not afraid to enter into dialogue with doubters and skeptics. His faith could stand the test of examination.

Jesus would be comfortable today on the university campus talking with young people whose minds are searching for the truth.

Our Lord found delight in the company of people celebrating

life's significant events. He loved life! He celebrated with other people. He was an honoree at a banquet at the house of Matthew the tax collector. He enjoyed fellowship in the homes of friends. He celebrated life in his carpenter's shop.

Henry Van Dyke captured the spirit of Christ as follows:

This is the gospel of labor!
Ring it, ye bells of the kirk.
The Lord of love came down from above,
To dwell with the men who work.

Jesus believed the gospel had social application. He always "went about doing good." He had a way of discovering human need. Watch the panorama unfold:

Sickness—he healed a diseased leper and made the lame man walk.

Guilt—he had pity on a woman accused of adultery and forgave her.

Hunger—he multiplied bread and fed the hungry multitudes.

Grief—he wept with Mary and Martha in sorrow over the death of their brother Lazarus and raised him from the dead.

Soul sickness—he had compassion on troubled souls and made them whole again.

Our master was known as the "suffering servant." He was willing to suffer vicariously for others. Even when his enemies nailed him to the cross, he prayed, "Father, forgive them; they don't understand what they are doing."

The servants of Christ are part of a great social organism. Sometimes they must suffer for the sins of others in order to bring about redemption.

Where is the action for me? For you?

Where worship takes place—adoration, praise, thanksgiving, confession, forgiveness, renewal.

At some center of learning—intellectual challenge, serious reflection, sorting out priorities.

Celebrating life—with family, friends, fellow-citizens.

Stooping to serve—the poor, the diseased, drug addicts, the invisibly wounded.

Sharing the sins—of burglars, rapists, leaders of violence.

God's Word

John heard in prison about the deeds of Christ. . . . Jesus said, "Go and tell John what you hear and see; The blind receive their sight and the lame walk, lepers are cleansed and the deaf hear, the dead are raised up, and the poor have good news preached to them. And blessed is he who takes no offense at me."

—Matthew 11:2,4-6

The Son of man came not to be served but to serve, and to give his life a ransom for many.

—Mark 10:45

If anyone wishes to be a follower of mine he must leave self behind; day after day he must take up his cross and come with me. Whoever cares for his own safety is lost; but if a man will let himself be lost for my sake, that man is safe.

—Luke 9:23–24, NEB

A Prayer

God of action,
Guide my feet where you are at work
Give me a clear view of human needs
Prick my conscience into restlessness
Inspire my heart into purposeful action
Strengthen my hands for effective work
Keep me anchored where your action is,
In the grace of Christ our Lord.

Amen.

25.
THE RIGHT TO BECOME

In his book *To Be Human Now* David O. Woodyard says that the challenge of our time is the burden "to be human now." He refers to W. H. Auden's Christmas Oratorio, *For the Time Being*. In the story the three Wise Men tell why they are following the star of the Nativity.

The first Wise Man:
    To discover how to be truthful now
    Is the reason I follow the star.
The second Wise Man:
    To discover how to be living now
    Is the reason I follow the star.
The third Wise Man:
    To discover how to be loving now
    Is the reason I follow the star.
The three Wise Men:
    To discover how to be human now
    Is the reason we follow this star.[1]

Within every man is the desire to become more than he is. In fact, he has the right to become the person God meant him to be.

Man is a paradox to himself. He has the ability to see visions, yet he often feels himself surrounded by darkness. He longs for the heights but finds himself falling into the depths.

Pascal in *Pensee's* gave this vivid description:

What a chimera (delusion) then is man!
What a novelty! What a monster, what a chaos,
What a contradiction, what a prodigy!
Judge of all things, imbecile worm of the earth;
Depository of truth, a sewer of uncertainty and error;
The pride and refuse of the universe.

In contrast Shakespeare (*Hamlet,* Act II) exults at the nature of man:

What a piece of work is a man!
How noble in reason!
How infinite in faculty!
In form and moving how express and admirable!
In action how like an angel,
In apprehension how like a god!

If man is to become what he has a right to become, he can neither take an attitude of hopeless pessimism nor an attitude of romantic optimism.

Paul the apostle was a restless person by nature. He was also a doggedly determined person. At first he rebelled against the gospel which really meant rebellion against Jesus Christ who came to achieve redemption and good news.

A great change came in Paul in his Damascus road experience. And he kept on changing—growing in attitude and capacity to achieve truth and to appropriate life's blessings.

The starting point to becoming is to acknowledge a sense of responsibility for oneself. Man is made for freedom but he can only be free as he exercises his humanity. Niebuhr reminds us "the great God has treated us as responsible beings."

The challenge "to become" requires self-awareness. To experience oneself is to realize that he has himself on his own hands. There is a certain amount of self-consciousness in being a person. Man must avoid becoming preoccupied with self-awareness, however.

To grow, to become, to mature, to respond to God's purpose, man must live with a certain openness to life. Openness to the world, to others, to God.

Openness requires humility, the desire to learn, and trust.

Pascal said:

Know thou, proud man,
What a paradox you are to yourself.
Humble yourself, weak reason;
Be silent, foolish nature;
Learn that man infinitely transcends man,
And learn from your master your true condition,
Of which you are ignorant. Hear God.

To become, man must accept himself:
With all his potentialities and noble ideals,
With his finite limitations and weaknesses,
With his self-centeredness, his faults and his sins.

In order to become his true self man must love himself. An extreme view of the doctrine of man's fall into sin often leads to the heresy of self-deprecation and even hatred of self.

What does it mean to love oneself? To love anyone is:
To be glad that he is alive.
To want a full and rich experience for him.
To value him as a person and not exploit him.
To be concerned with his welfare and seek to meet his needs.[2]

Carroll Wise goes on to say that this includes loving oneself. "To accept and affirm oneself as a person, to seek full and rich experience for oneself, to have self-respect, to be concerned for and do what is necessary for our own welfare; these attitudes are necessary to health and well being."

Jesus said the second great commandment is "to love one's neighbor as oneself." This kind of love is to be distinguished from selfishness or self-centeredness. It means the fulfilment of self so that one may more fully give his love in his ministry to others.

In order to become a whole person one must learn to live in relationship with others. He must love his neighbor as himself. No one achieves self-actualization by isolation, but only in relationship.

Man can become truly human now, as God created him to be, when he hears and heeds the higher voice of God. In order to become, man must see his life as vocation, as calling according to the purpose of God.

Christian vocation means that man is called of God to accept redemption, to be Christian in his living, to witness to the good news of God's grace, and to serve his fellowman with all his abilities.

The philosopher-physician Paracelsus long ago affirmed: "Man carries the stars within himself." This is true only when he opens his eyes of faith to the vision of God's eternal Star.

Man's path may not always be flooded with light, but honest faith will always provide enough light to steer by.

The poet Henry Vaughan (1622–95) spoke of the light seen by Nicodemus that "made him know his God by sight." He wrote:

There is in God (someway)
A deep but dazzling darkness; as men here
Say it is late and dusky because they
See not all clear;
Oh, for that night! where I in him
Might live invisible and dim.

God's Word

To all who did receive him, to these who have yielded him their allegiance he gave the right to become the children of God.

—John 1:12, NEB

I do not consider myself to "have arrived," spiritually, nor do I consider myself already perfect, but I keep going on, grasping ever more firmly that purpose for which Christ Jesus grasped me.

—Philippians 3:12, Phillips

We are not meant to remain as children. . . . but we are meant to hold firmly to the truth in love, and to grow up in every way into Christ, the head.

—Ephesians 4:14–15, Phillips.

A Prayer

O God, I am so stubborn,
And, yet, you gave me this determined nature.
I'm not easily changed,
And I thank you for that.
But I want to change for the better,
For what is ultimate and eternal.
Help me really to forget
My stupid blunders and selfish ambitions
And bad interpersonal relations
And false reasonings
And especially my rebellion against you.
Give me enabling grace to press on
Toward the ultimate goal in Christ Jesus.

Amen.

NOTES

1. David O. Woodyard, *To Be Human Now*. (Philadelphia: Westminster Press, 1969), p. 8.

2. Carroll A. Wise, *Psychiatry and the Bible* (New York: Harper and Bros., 1956), p. 117.